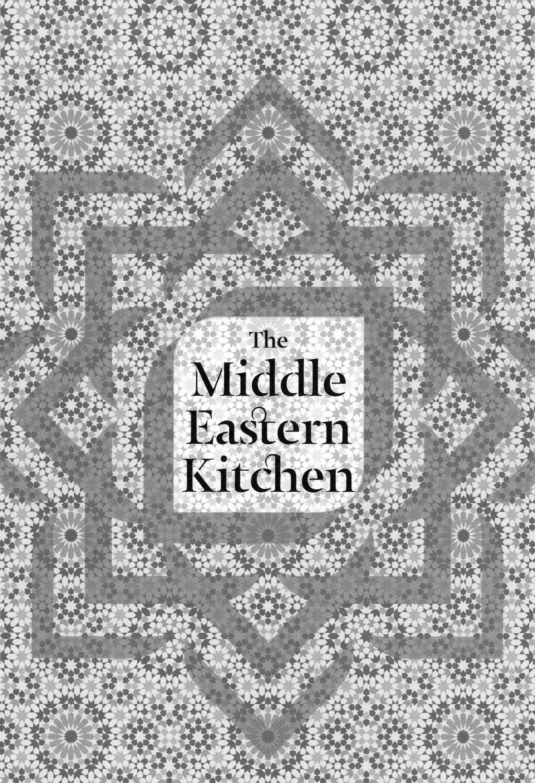

The
Middle
Eastern
Kitchen

The
Middle
Eastern
Kitchen

New recipes by Rukmini Iyer

First published by Parragon Books Ltd in 2016
LOVE FOOD is an imprint of Parragon Books Ltd

Parragon Books Ltd
Chartist House
15–17 Trim Street
Bath BA1 1HA, UK
www.parragon.com/lovefood

ISBN: 978-1-4748-0409-7

Printed in China

New recipes and food styling: Rukmini Iyer
Created and produced by Pene Parker and Becca Spry
Author portrait photograph: Simon Brown
Background images, pattern images and image on
page 48 supplied courtesy of iStock and Shutterstock

Notes for the reader

This book uses both metric and imperial
measurements. Follow the same units of
measurement throughout; do not mix metric
and imperial. All spoon measurements are level:
teaspoons are assumed to be 5 ml, and tablespoons
are assumed to be 15 ml. Unless otherwise stated,
milk is assumed to be full fat, eggs and individual
fruits and vegetables are medium, pepper is freshly
ground black pepper and all root vegetables should
be peeled prior to use.

Garnishes, decorations and serving suggestions
are all optional and not necessarily included in
the recipe ingredients or method. The times given
are an approximate guide only. Preparation times
differ according to the techniques used by different
people and the cooking times may also vary from
those given.

For best results, use a food thermometer when
cooking meat. Check the latest government
guidelines for current advice.

Contents

The Middle Eastern Kitchen

From Turkey's yogurt, feta, honey and pomegranates to North Africa's ras el hanout, dates and rosewater, the variety of ingredients in the Middle East is equalled only by the diversity of the region's dishes. The food of Iran, formerly Persia, is perhaps the most refined of the area, with its layered spicing and famed jewelled rice dishes. However, Moroccan and Tunisian classics are among the most popular today, including spicy tagines and fiery harissa. They act as a gateway to the wider region. Iraq, Syria, Lebanon, Jordan, Palestine, Israel, Turkey and the Yemen all have a wealth of dishes and ingredients reflected in the recipes in this book.

The Middle Eastern cook has an abundance of fresh produce to draw on. There are river and saltwater fish, armfuls of fresh herbs such as mint and coriander, sunny Mediterranean vegetables and a variety of meats, such as lamb and chicken (see page 49), as well as grains, such as bulgur and freekeh. Nuts such as pistachios and almonds are used to thicken sauces and add texture, with walnuts popular in Iran and Turkey and pine nuts in Syria and Egypt. Dates, dried apricots, barberries and raisins bring a sweetness to savoury dishes — a popular combination throughout the region.

All these ingredients can be combined and cooked in a dizzying variety of ways. Street food is quickly grilled over charcoal braziers, a home cook may painstakingly roll, stuff and deep-fry pastries, rich tagines are left to simmer slowly for hours, and crunchy, vibrant vegetables are quickly thrown together in salads.

Spices, from complex blends to a simple sprinkling of sumac before serving, bring depth and flavour to a wide range of dishes. Pickles and preserves (see pages 166–169) add flavour and texture to a meal. Luckily for the home cook, the wide availability of these exotic ingredients means that Middle Eastern cooking is accessible outside the region.

Most of the dishes in this book are simple enough to throw together for a quick, flavour-packed week-night dinner. For weekend cooking, there are plenty of easy, slow-cooked stews and tagines, and the more hands-on kibbeh and small pies are great for an afternoon of adventurous assembly-line cooking.

For special occasions, you can combine dishes from different chapters to create a sharing feast for friends. A particularly good combination is Griddled Aubergine with Pomegranate, Coriander & Yogurt (page 78), Chicken Kebabs with Za'atar Dip (page 24), Lamb Kofte with Yogurt & Mint Dip (page 66), Fattoush (page 134) and Classic Tabbouleh (page 120), all of which can be prepared in advance. If you're having a lot of people over, a big pot of Persian Jewelled Rice (page 88), Fesenjan Chicken & Walnut Stew (page 40) and Pomegranate Salad with Herbs & Pistachios (page 142) makes the perfect feast to feed a large crowd. Or as an alternative to a Sunday roast, try the Ras el Hanout, Garlic & Thyme Roast Leg of Lamb (page 82).

Once you're confident with the simple techniques and spice blends in the book, you can modify the recipes to suit your own favourite vegetable or herb combinations. Use coriander instead of flat-leaf parsley, substitute ras el hanout for za'atar in a spice rub, add more or less chilli to a sauce depending on your preference, and make the dishes your own. In Middle Eastern cooking, as with all recipes, taste as you go along; the perfect combination of lemon juice, sea salt and freshly ground black pepper, if you like to use them, will vary from cook to cook. Taste, season, then taste again before serving so you can adjust the dishes to suit your palate.

Middle Eastern recipes evolve as you cook them, depending on your taste and the ingredients you have to hand. The region's food and its rich cultural history have similarly evolved into the complex, diverse and fascinating culinary landscape of today.

Meze

Beetroot Falafel with Pittas

PREP: 1 hour
COOK: 35 minutes
RISE: 55 minutes
SERVES: 4

800 g/1 lb 12 oz canned chickpeas
  in water, drained and rinsed

1 red onion, finely chopped

2 garlic cloves, thinly sliced

1 tsp cumin seeds, crushed

1 tsp sumac

1 tsp baking powder

175 g/6 oz (about 2) raw beetroot,
  coarsely grated

large pinch of sea salt

large pinch of pepper

3 tbsp olive oil, to brush

8 lettuce leaves, shredded, to serve

Wholemeal pitta breads

250 g/9 oz wholemeal flour,
  plus 2½ tsp to dust

½ tsp sea salt flakes, crushed

1 tsp dark muscovado sugar

1 tsp easy-blend dried yeast

1 tsp cumin seeds, crushed

1 tbsp olive oil

150–175 ml/5–6 fl oz warm water

Tzatziki

½ cucumber, halved, deseeded
  and finely chopped

150 g/5½ oz Greek-style natural yogurt

2 tbsp finely chopped fresh mint

pinch of sea salt

pinch of pepper

Traditionally deep-fried, these ruby-coloured falafel are flavoured with cumin and sumac then roasted. Serve in home-made pittas with spoonfuls of tzatziki and lettuce.

1. For the pittas, mix the flour, salt, sugar, yeast and cumin together in a bowl. Add the oil, then gradually mix in enough warm water to make a soft dough. Dust a work surface with 1 teaspoon of flour. Knead the dough on the surface for 5 minutes, or until smooth and elastic. Return it to the bowl, cover it with a clean tea towel and put it in a warm place for 45 minutes, or until doubled in size.

2. When you are almost ready to cook, preheat the oven to 220°C/425°F/Gas Mark 7. Dust a work surface with 1 teaspoon of flour. Knead the dough gently, then cut it into four pieces and roll out each piece into an oval about the size of your hand. Leave to rise for 10 minutes.

3. Lightly dust two baking sheets with the remaining flour, then put them in the oven for 5 minutes. Add the breads to the hot baking sheets and bake for 5–10 minutes, or until puffed up and lightly browned. Wrap them in a clean tea towel to keep them soft.

4. Meanwhile, put the chickpeas in a food processor or blender, in small batches, and whizz into a coarse paste, scraping down the sides of the goblet several times using a spatula. Tip them into a bowl. Add the red onion, garlic, cumin, sumac, baking powder and beetroot, season with the salt and pepper, then mix together using a fork.

5. Spoon the mixture into 20 mounds on a chopping board, then squeeze them into balls. Brush a large roasting tin with a little oil, then heat it in the oven for 5 minutes. Add the falafel and brush well with more oil. Roast for 20–25 minutes, turning once or twice, until browned and cooked through; break one open and taste to check.

6. Meanwhile, to make the tzatziki, put the cucumber, yogurt and mint in a bowl, season with the salt and pepper and mix well.

7. To serve, split the warm pittas open, stuff with the lettuce, tzatziki and falafel and serve with any remaining tzatziki.

Cook's tip: *Make a double quantity of pitta breads and freeze half the cooked breads in a plastic bag. Defrost at room temperature for 1 hour, then warm in a frying pan for 2 minutes on each side.*

This simple, traditional Levantine recipe of crispy meat-stuffed pitta breads is a perfect snack. You'll be hard-pressed to get any from the oven to the table – they're too delicious not to be eaten standing up, straight from the baking sheet. For a vegetarian alternative, substitute finely chopped chestnut mushrooms for the mince.

Arayes

PREP: 25 minutes
COOK: 1 hour
SERVES: 4

3 tbsp olive oil

1 tsp cumin seeds

½ onion, finely chopped

2 garlic cloves, finely chopped

1 tsp ground ginger

1 tsp ground coriander

1 tsp ground cumin

250 g/9 oz fresh beef or lamb mince

2 large tomatoes, finely chopped

3 large pinches of sea salt flakes

large pinch of pepper

4 tbsp finely chopped fresh
   flat-leaf parsley

4 wholemeal pitta breads

1. Heat 1 tablespoon of the oil in a frying pan over a low heat. Add the cumin seeds and fry for 1 minute, or until aromatic. Add the onion and garlic, increase the heat to medium–high, and fry for 10 minutes, or until golden.

2. Reduce the heat to low, add the ginger, coriander and ground cumin, and fry for 1–2 minutes, stirring constantly. Add the mince, increase the heat to medium–high, and fry for 10 minutes, or until it is well browned, breaking it up using a wooden spoon.

3. Add the tomatoes and a large pinch of salt and pepper, stir, then cover and reduce the heat to low. Cook for 20 minutes, then stir in most of the parsley. Preheat the oven to 180°C/350°F/Gas Mark 4.

4. Halve or quarter the pitta breads and carefully open the pockets. Stuff each pocket with a heaped tablespoon of the filling, then place on a baking sheet. Brush each pocket on both sides with the remaining 2 tablespoons of oil and sprinkle with a large pinch of salt. Bake for 20 minutes, or until golden and crispy.

5. Serve immediately, scattered with the remaining parsley and a large pinch of salt.

Cook's tip: *The meat filling can be cooked up to a day in advance if covered and refrigerated once cool.*

A plate of stuffed vine leaves is one of the most popular meze in the Middle East. The leaves can be stuffed with meat, rice or vegetables, or a combination of all three. You could easily make a vegetarian version of this recipe by omitting the mince and doubling the tomato.

Stuffed Vine Leaves

PREP: 45 minutes
COOK: 1½ hours
SERVES: 6

200 g/7 oz drained vine leaves
  (see Cook's tip)
100 g/3½ oz basmati rice
about 750 ml/1¼ pints boiling water
2 garlic cloves, finely chopped
1 onion, finely chopped
2 tomatoes, finely chopped
200 g/7 oz fresh beef or lamb mince
2 tsp sea salt flakes
1 tbsp finely chopped fresh oregano
1 tbsp finely chopped fresh mint
1 lemon, thinly sliced

1. Separate the vine leaves and put them in a large bowl. Cover with water, then rinse with three changes of water. Cover with more water and soak for 25 minutes, then drain well.

2. Meanwhile, rinse the rice in several changes of water. Tip it into a saucepan and cover with 3–4 cm/1¼–1¾ inches boiling water. Parboil for 3 minutes, then drain well.

3. Tip the rice into a medium bowl. Add the garlic, onion, tomatoes, mince, salt, oregano and mint, and mix well using your hands.

4. Put a steamer basket in a large saucepan. Line the basket with any torn vine leaves plus the smallest ones. Lay half the lemon slices on the leaves.

5. Lay one of the bigger vine leaves vein side-up on a work surface. Put a heaped teaspoon of filling in the centre. Fold the top of the leaf over the filling, then fold over the two sides before rolling up the leaf like a cigar, with the folded edge underneath.

6. Put the stuffed vine leaf in the steamer basket. Repeat with the remaining leaves and filling. Your basket should be full, with tightly packed layers. Finish with a layer of lemon slices.

7. Pour 400 ml/14 fl oz water into the saucepan, cover the steamer with a tightly fitting lid and bring to the boil. Reduce the heat to very low and steam for 1 hour 25 minutes, or until the rice and mince have cooked through and the vine leaves have softened.

8. These are best served hot, but can also be served cold.

Cook's tip: Vacuum-packed vine leaves are easier to work with than those from jars.

These fiery Tunisian-inspired prawn skewers are great as part of a meze feast or as a starter. Serve them with a simple salad such as Classic Tabbouleh (page 120) or Chickpea, Halloumi, Red Onion & Coriander Salad (page 100). You will need four wooden skewers.

Griddled Harissa Prawn Skewers

PREP: 15 minutes
MARINATE: 30 minutes
COOK: 6 minutes
SERVES: 4

250 g/9 oz raw king prawns (approx. 6 per person), peeled and deveined, defrosted if frozen

2 tsp rose harissa

1 tsp fine sea salt

2 garlic cloves, finely chopped

4 tbsp finely chopped fresh coriander

2 tbsp olive oil

pinch of sea salt flakes

1 lemon, cut into wedges, to serve

1. Mix the prawns, rose harissa, fine sea salt, garlic and half the coriander together in a large bowl. Cover and marinate in the refrigerator for 30 minutes.

2. Soak four wooden skewers in water for 20 minutes, then drain well. Thread the prawns onto the skewers and brush them lightly with the oil.

3. Heat a griddle pan or heavy-based frying pan over a high heat until smoking hot. Lay the skewers on the pan, reduce the heat slightly and cook for 4–6 minutes, or until pink and cooked through, turning halfway.

4. Serve the skewers immediately, scattered with the remaining coriander and the sea salt flakes, with lemon wedges for squeezing over.

Cook's tip: *For extra flavour, add the grated zest of an unwaxed lemon to the marinade. Don't add lemon juice as it will 'cook' the prawns before they go on the griddle.*

Kibbeh

PREP: 40 minutes
SOAK: 30 minutes
CHILL: 1 hour
COOK: 1 hour
MAKES: 12

100 g/3½ oz bulgur wheat

½ onion, roughly chopped

200 g/7 oz fresh lamb mince

1 tsp ground cumin

pinch of pepper

2 tsp sea salt flakes

1 litre/1¾ pints vegetable oil

Filling

40 g/1½ oz pine nuts

1 tbsp olive oil

½ onion, finely chopped

½ tbsp ground cinnamon

½ tbsp ground allspice

½ tbsp ground cumin

200 g/7 oz fresh lamb mince

3 tbsp finely chopped fresh
   coriander

1 tbsp Greek-style natural yogurt

pinch of sea salt flakes

pinch of pepper

Cook's tip: *If the kibbeh turn brown too quickly when being fried, the oil is too hot and the outside will burn before the inside is cooked. Let the oil cool a little before cooking. Don't leave the pan unattended, don't fill it more than half-full, keep it towards the back of the stove, have the heat no higher than medium, and don't overcrowd the pan or the oil may bubble over.*

Take your time when shaping the delicate outer kibbeh shell before stuffing it with spiced lamb or beef mince. It requires patience, but you will be rewarded with meltingly delicious meze.

1. For the shell, rinse the bulgur wheat in several changes of water, then leave it to soak for 30 minutes. Drain well, squeeze out any excess water, then tip into a food processor. Add the onion, mince, cumin and pepper, then pulse until well mixed. Tip into a bowl, cover, then chill in the refrigerator while you make the filling.

2. For the filling, toast the pine nuts in a frying pan over a low heat for 2–3 minutes. Tip into a bowl and set aside.

3. Heat the olive oil in the pan over a medium–high heat. Add the onion and fry for 10 minutes, stirring occasionally. Reduce the heat to medium–low, stir in the cinnamon, allspice and cumin, and fry for 1–2 minutes, or until aromatic. Add the mince, increase the heat to medium–high, and fry for 10 minutes, or until well browned, breaking it up using a wooden spoon. Mix in the coriander, toasted pine nuts, yogurt, salt and pepper. Set aside to cool.

4. For the shell, mix the salt into the bulgur mixture. (To check for seasoning, fry a little of the mixture until cooked.) Divide the mixture into 12 and roll into balls using wet hands. Press each ball down gently over your thumb to form a deep 'cup'. Using your thumb and index finger, and your other hand to rotate the cup, flatten out the sides as thinly as possible without breaking the shell.

5. Fill each 'cup' with a heaped tablespoon of the filling, then press the top closed, patting the mixture down into the shape of a lemon. Transfer to a plate. Repeat until you've made all the kibbeh, then cover and refrigerate for 1 hour, or until ready to cook.

6. Pour the vegetable oil into a large, deep-sided saucepan until no more than half-full. Heat over a medium heat for 5–10 minutes, or until a cube of bread dropped in sizzles immediately and turns golden within a minute (about 180°C/350°F if you are using a thermometer). Working in batches of three to four, fry the kibbeh for 5 minutes, or until golden brown and cooked through. Drain on kitchen paper and serve hot.

Stuffed roast vegetables are popular throughout the Middle East. These Turkish-inspired stuffed tomatoes are a perfect vegetarian option.

Stuffed Roast Tomatoes with Pine Nuts, Feta & Parsley

PREP: 15 minutes
COOK: 30 minutes
SERVES: 4

1 tbsp olive oil

1 small red onion, finely chopped

1 garlic clove, finely chopped

8 large tomatoes

60 g/2¼ oz feta cheese, crumbled

30 g/1 oz pine nuts

6 tbsp finely chopped fresh flat-leaf parsley

pinch of sea salt

pinch of pepper

1. Preheat the oven to 180°C/350°F/Gas Mark 4. Heat the oil in a saucepan over a medium heat. Add the red onion and garlic and cook for 5–10 minutes, or until translucent. Tip into a large bowl and leave to cool.

2. Meanwhile, using a small, sharp knife, cut a 2.5-cm/1-inch diameter circle around the stem of each tomato to form a lid. Using a small spoon, scoop out the seeds and discard.

3. Mix the feta, pine nuts and parsley into the onion and garlic, and season with the salt and pepper. Stuff the tomatoes with this mixture, pressing it down well using the back of a spoon.

4. Place a 'lid' on each tomato and put them in a shallow baking dish. Roast for 20 minutes, or until completely softened. Serve warm.

Cook's tip: *Red peppers are also good stuffed. Choose small peppers and remove the seeds, then soften them in the oven at 180°C/350°F/Gas Mark 4 for 5–10 minutes before filling and baking them.*

Chicken
Kebabs with
Za'atar Dip
page 24

The meltingly soft marinated chicken contrasts beautifully with the red onions and red peppers in these wonderfully spicy kebabs. You will need eight wooden skewers for this recipe.

Chicken Kebabs with Za'atar Dip

PREP: 20 minutes
MARINATE: 1 hour
COOK: 25 minutes
SERVES: 4

1 garlic clove, crushed

grated zest and juice of ½ unwaxed lemon

½ tsp ground cumin

½ tsp ground ginger

1 tsp cayenne pepper

¼ tsp ground turmeric

50 g/1¾ oz natural yogurt

1 tsp sea salt flakes, crushed

2 large skinless, boneless chicken
   breasts, about 150 g/5½ oz each, cut
   into 2.5-cm/1-inch cubes

1 red pepper, deseeded and cut into
   2.5-cm/1-inch chunks

1 red onion, cut into 2.5-cm/1-inch chunks

1 tbsp olive oil

Za'atar dip
2 tbsp olive oil
1 tbsp za'atar spice

1. Mix the garlic, lemon zest and juice, cumin, ginger, cayenne, turmeric, yogurt and most of the salt together in a large bowl. Add the chicken and mix until well coated. Cover and marinate in the refrigerator for at least 1 hour, or overnight.

2. Meanwhile, soak the eight wooden skewers in water for 20 minutes, then drain well. Preheat the oven to 200°C/400°F/Gas Mark 6. Line a roasting tin with foil.

3. Thread the chicken cubes onto the skewers, alternating with the red pepper and red onion chunks, and place them in the prepared roasting tin. If you have leftover onion and pepper, put them in the tin too. Brush the chicken and vegetables with the oil, then roast at the top of the oven for 25 minutes, or until the chicken is cooked through, golden and slightly charred.

4. For the dip, mix the oil and za'atar together in a small bowl.

5. Leave the kebabs to rest for 5 minutes. Serve, sprinkled with the remaining salt, with the za'atar dip.

› **Pictured on previous page**

Cook's tip: To griddle the kebabs, heat a griddle pan over a medium–high heat until hot. Lay the skewers in the pan and cook for 15–20 minutes, or until the chicken is cooked through, golden and slightly charred, turning regularly.

With an irresistible balance of spice, sweetness and salt, and seared crispy skin, these chicken wings make a very moreish snack. They're perfect as part of a meze meal or for a lazy dinner.

Roast Chicken Wings with Sumac, Lemon & Garlic

PREP: 25 minutes
COOK: 25 minutes
SERVES: 4

2 tbsp olive oil

1 tbsp runny honey

2 garlic cloves, crushed

3 tsp sumac

2 tsp sea salt flakes, crushed

grated zest of 1 unwaxed lemon, plus
  1 lemon, cut into wedges, to serve

500 g/1 lb 2 oz chicken wings,
  cut into drumettes and wingettes

4 tbsp Greek-style natural yogurt,
  to serve

1. Preheat the oven to 220°C/425°F/Gas Mark 7. Mix the oil, honey, garlic, sumac, salt and lemon zest together in a large roasting tin. Add the chicken and mix until well coated.

2. Roast the chicken at the top of the oven for 25 minutes, or until cooked through and slightly charred with a crispy skin, shaking the tin halfway through cooking to turn the pieces. Push a skewer into a chicken piece; the meat should no longer be pink and the juices should be clear and piping hot.

3. Leave the chicken to rest for 5 minutes. Serve with the Greek yogurt and lemon wedges for squeezing over.

› **Pictured overleaf**

Cook's tip: A chicken wing is comprised of the tip, drumette and wingette. The tip is usually discarded, although in Asia it is often regarded as a delicacy. The wingette is the flat middle part and the drumette (which looks like a miniature drumstick) is the upper part. To separate them, wiggle the joint backwards and forwards so you feel where it is connected, then cut through the hinge using the heel of the knife, pushing down hard.

Roast
Chicken Wings
with Sumac,
Lemon & Garlic
page 25

This is a classic Iranian frittata, filled with fresh herbs and walnuts. It makes a lovely meze dish or light lunch served with salad.

Persian Herb Frittata

PREP: 15 minutes
COOK: 10 minutes
SERVES: 2

6 eggs

2 tbsp finely chopped fresh dill

6 tbsp finely chopped fresh flat-leaf parsley

6 tbsp finely chopped fresh coriander

2 tbsp finely chopped fresh mint

2 garlic cloves, crushed

1 tbsp plain flour

¼ tsp ground turmeric

large pinch of sea salt

large pinch of pepper

20 g/¾ oz butter

1 tbsp olive oil

30 g/1 oz walnuts, chopped

1 spring onion, thinly sliced, to garnish

1. Preheat the oven to 180°C/350°F/Gas Mark 4. Crack the eggs into a large bowl. Add the herbs, garlic, flour, turmeric, salt and pepper, then whisk well.

2. Heat the butter with the oil in a large, heavy-based, ovenproof frying pan over a medium–high heat until foaming. As soon as it stops foaming, pour in the egg mixture, reduce the heat to medium–low and cook for 5 minutes.

3. Scatter the walnuts over the frittata, then transfer the frying pan to the oven and bake for 5 minutes, or until cooked through.

4. Using oven gloves, turn the frittata out onto a plate. Scatter with the spring onion, then cut into wedges and serve.

Cook's tip: You can make a frittata with most soft herbs, mixed to suit your taste. Basil, tarragon, chervil and chives all work well.

Crispy Sumac Squid Rings with Lemon Yogurt Dip

PREP: 25 minutes
CHILL: 1 hour
COOK: 15 minutes
SERVES: 4

200 g/7 oz squid tubes, cleaned
  and cut into rings

approx. 300 ml/10 fl oz full-fat milk

50 g/1¾ oz rice breadcrumbs

1½ tsp sumac

2 pinches of sea salt flakes

1 egg, lightly beaten

3 tbsp olive oil

1 lemon, cut into wedges, to serve

Lemon yogurt dip

150 g/5½ oz Greek-style natural yogurt

juice of ½ lemon

These squid rings are crispy on the outside and perfectly tender within. Serve them hot as a snack with drinks, or as part of a bigger meze meal.

1. Put the squid in a shallow bowl and pour over just enough of the milk to cover. Cover and chill in the refrigerator for 1 hour, to soften.

2. Meanwhile, for the dip, mix the yogurt and lemon juice together in a bowl. Cover and chill in the refrigerator until needed.

3. Put the rice breadcrumbs, sumac and a pinch of salt on a plate and mix well. Put the egg in a shallow bowl.

4. Strain the squid through a colander and discard the milk. Give the colander a good shake to remove any excess liquid.

5. Lay a large sheet of baking paper on a work surface and line a plate with kitchen paper. Dip each squid ring in the egg, then in the sumac crumbs, then place on the baking paper.

6. Heat half the oil in a wok or large frying pan over a medium–high heat. Working in batches, fry the squid for 3–4 minutes, or until crisp and cooked, turning halfway through, then transfer to the prepared plate. Add more oil to the pan as needed.

7. Serve the squid hot, scattered with a pinch of salt, with the yogurt dip and lemon wedges for squeezing over.

Cook's tip: *If rice breadcrumbs are not available, use panko breadcrumbs instead.*

Falafel Pitta Pockets with Tahini Dressing

PREP: 25 minutes
COOK: 12 minutes
SERVES: 4

1 shallot, quartered

2 garlic cloves

400 g/14 oz canned chickpeas in water, drained and rinsed

6 tbsp roughly chopped fresh flat-leaf parsley

1 tsp ground coriander

1 tsp ground cumin

½ tsp sea salt flakes

pinch of cayenne pepper

2 tbsp olive oil

2 tbsp plain flour

½ tsp baking powder

2–4 tbsp rapeseed oil, for frying

Tahini dressing

2 tbsp tahini

juice of 1 lemon

2–3 tbsp water

½ tsp sea salt flakes

⅛ tsp pepper

⅛ tsp cayenne pepper

To serve

4 pitta breads

1 romaine lettuce heart, shredded

1 large tomato, thinly sliced

½ cucumber, thinly sliced

16 Kalamata olives

4 fresh mint sprigs

This popular Middle Eastern street food is easy to make and usually eaten as a meze starter or lunch. Serve hot, fresh from the pan.

1. Preheat the oven to 200°C/400°F/Gas Mark 6. Put the shallot and garlic in a food processor and pulse a few times, until chopped. Add the chickpeas, parsley, coriander, cumin, salt, cayenne, olive oil and flour, and whizz to a chunky purée. Add the baking powder and pulse once.

2. For the tahini dressing, mix all the ingredients together in a small bowl, adjusting the water content until you have the consistency you like. Wrap the pitta breads in foil and place them in the oven.

3. Line a plate with kitchen paper. Make walnut-sized balls out of the chickpea mixture, then flatten them into 5-mm/¼-inch-thick patties. Heat 2 tablespoons of the rapeseed oil in a large frying pan over a medium–high heat until hot. Working in batches, fry the patties for 3–4 minutes, or until well browned, turning halfway through, then transfer to the prepared plate. Add more oil to the pan as needed.

4. Slice the pitta breads in half. Stuff each half with two to three falafels, lettuce, tomato and cucumber, and drizzle with the dressing. Serve two halves per person with olives and a mint sprig.

Cook's tip: *This recipe works just as well with wholemeal pittas. You can try making your own or buy from a local bakery.*

Soups, Stews & Tagines

Broad beans are popular in the Middle East, and in this fresh, summery soup the mint brings out all their flavour.

Broad Bean & Mint Soup

PREP: 20 minutes
COOK: 15 minutes
SERVES: 4

1 kg/2 lb 4 oz broad beans in their pods
   (300 g/10½ oz podded weight), podded
2 tbsp olive oil
1 onion, finely chopped
400 ml/14 fl oz hot vegetable stock
2 garlic cloves, finely chopped
grated zest and juice of ½ unwaxed lemon
25 g/1 oz fresh mint leaves
pinch of sea salt
pinch of pepper
4 tbsp Greek-style natural yogurt

1. Put the beans in a heatproof bowl and pour over just enough boiling water to cover them. Drain them well and immediately plunge them into a bowl of cold water. Peel off and discard the outer skins and set the double-podded beans aside.

2. Meanwhile, heat the oil in a large saucepan over a low heat. Add the onion, cover and cook for 10 minutes, or until translucent, stirring occasionally. Add the beans, reserving a small handful, stir briefly, then pour in 300 ml/10 fl oz of the stock. Bring to the boil, then simmer for 2 minutes, or until the beans are tender.

3. Stir in the garlic, lemon zest and half the mint. Whizz in a food processor, or using a hand-held blender, until smooth. Check the consistency and if you prefer a thinner soup, mix in a little or all of the reserved stock. Stir in the lemon juice, salt and pepper.

4. Pour the soup into four shallow bowls. Swirl a tablespoon of yogurt into each bowl, then scatter with the reserved beans and tear over the remaining mint leaves.

Cook's tip: This soup is lovely served hot. However, it is equally good chilled as a refresher for a hot summer's day. In step four, leave it to cool to room temperature, then refrigerate.

Kofte, or meatballs cooked in broth, are popular throughout the Middle East. Turkey, Syria and Iran all have variations on different types of meatball served in a clear broth or soup with vegetables. Here, they gain extra depth of flavour from the treacly pomegranate molasses.

Lebanese Seven-spice Beef Kofte Broth

PREP: 25 minutes
COOK: 20 minutes
SERVES: 4

500 g/1 lb 2 oz fresh beef mince

2 garlic cloves, finely chopped

2 tbsp finely chopped fresh coriander

1 heaped tbsp pomegranate molasses

1 tbsp runny honey

1 tsp sea salt flakes, plus a pinch

1 tbsp olive oil

800 ml/1 pint 7 fl oz hot chicken stock

½ savoy cabbage, cored and
   thickly sliced or cut into triangles

pinch of pepper

Lebanese seven-spice

1 tbsp pepper

1 tbsp ground allspice

1 tbsp ground cinnamon

1 tsp freshly grated nutmeg

1 tsp ground coriander

1 tsp ground cloves

1 tsp ground ginger

1. Preheat the oven to 180°C/350°F/Gas Mark 4. For the Lebanese seven-spice, mix all the spices together in a small bowl.

2. Mix the mince, garlic, coriander, pomegranate molasses, honey, 3 tablespoons of seven-spice and 1 teaspoon of salt together in a large bowl (store any remaining seven-spice in a sealed container for up to one month). Use your hands to work the flavourings into the meat. Divide the mixture into walnut-sized pieces and roll them into about 20 small kofte.

3. Heat the oil in a large frying pan over a medium–high heat until hot. Working in two batches, fry the kofte for 4 minutes, or until golden brown and crisp, turning halfway through, then transfer to a large, lidded casserole dish.

4. Add the hot stock to the casserole dish and bring to the boil. Cover, then bake for 10 minutes. Stir in the cabbage and bake for a further 5 minutes, or until the kofte are cooked.

5. Taste the broth and season with a pinch of salt and pepper. Serve the kofte and cabbage in deep bowls with the hot broth poured over.

Cook's tip: *For a more substantial dish, serve with some fluffy white rice.*

Chicken Soup with Chilli, Mint & Couscous

PREP: 20 minutes
COOK: 1¾ hours
SERVES: 4

1 tbsp olive oil

2 onions, finely chopped

1 red chilli, deseeded and finely chopped

1 tsp ground cumin

1 tsp paprika

1 tsp granulated sugar

2 tsp dried mint

1 tbsp tomato purée

100 g/3½ oz couscous

3 tbsp finely chopped fresh coriander, to garnish

1 lemon, cut into wedges, to serve

Stock

1 ready-to-cook chicken, weighing 1.3 kg/3 lb

1 onion, quartered

1 unwaxed lemon, quartered

15 g/½ oz fresh parsley stalks

1 tsp coriander seeds

1 cinnamon stick

pinch of sea salt

pinch of pepper

The broth for this classic Middle Eastern soup is made with a whole chicken, which is then torn into strips before being added back to the soup.

1. For the stock, put the chicken, onion, lemon, parsley stalks, coriander seeds and cinnamon stick in a deep saucepan and pour in just enough water to cover. Bring to the boil, then reduce the heat to medium–low, cover and simmer for 1 hour, or until the chicken is almost falling off the bone. To check it is cooked, pierce the thickest part of the thigh with a skewer. Any juices should be piping hot and clear with no traces of red or pink.

2. Transfer the chicken to a large plate and leave to cool slightly. Meanwhile, simmer the broth until it has reduced to about 1.2 litres/2 pints. Season with the salt and pepper, then sieve into a jug. Remove the skin from the chicken and tear the flesh into strips.

3. Heat the oil in a heavy-based saucepan over a medium heat. Add the onions and chilli and fry for 2–3 minutes, stirring often. Stir in the cumin, paprika, sugar, mint and tomato purée, then pour in the broth. Bring to the boil, then gradually stir in the couscous. Reduce the heat to medium–low and simmer for 15 minutes. Stir in the cooked chicken strips and simmer for 5 minutes.

4. Serve the soup in shallow bowls, garnished with the coriander, with lemon wedges for squeezing over.

Lamb Tagine
with Sticky Dates & Olives

PREP: 20 minutes
MARINATE: 4 hours
COOK: 2½ hours
SERVES: 8

1.8 kg/4 lb boned lamb shoulder, trimmed of fat and cut into 4-cm/1½-inch cubes

4 tbsp olive oil

250 g/9 oz stoned dates

250 g/9 oz stoned black olives

750 ml/1¼ pints red wine

10 garlic cloves

6 tbsp finely chopped fresh coriander

Dry marinade

2 large onions, grated

4 garlic cloves, crushed

1 red chilli, deseeded and finely chopped

1 tsp paprika

2 tsp ground cumin

1 tsp ground ginger

1 tsp pepper

Couscous

800 g/1 lb 12 oz couscous

grated zest of 1 unwaxed lemon

1 tbsp fresh thyme leaves

A rich tagine made with tender lamb and sweet dates.

1. Mix all the marinade ingredients together in a casserole dish, then stir in the lamb. Cover and marinate in the refrigerator for 4 hours.

2. Preheat the oven to 150°C/300°F/Gas Mark 2. Remove the lamb from the refrigerator. Mix in the oil, dates, olives, wine and garlic, and cover. Bake for 2½ hours, or until the lamb is meltingly tender, removing the lid for the last 30 minutes of cooking.

3. Put the couscous in a shallow heatproof bowl, pour over just enough boiling water to cover, then leave for 10 minutes. Mix in the lemon zest and thyme, and fluff up using a fork. Stir most of the coriander into the tagine and serve, garnished with the remaining coriander, with the couscous.

This classic Persian feast of chicken cooked in walnut sauce is perfect for feeding a crowd on a special occasion. The chicken is slow-cooked until it almost falls apart, and the rich sauce gains body and flavour from the combination of ground walnuts and pomegranate molasses. In the north of Iran, this dish, or *khoresh*, is made using duck or game instead of chicken. Serve with Persian Jewelled Rice (page 88).

Fesenjan Chicken & Walnut Stew

PREP: 30 minutes
COOK: 3 hours
SERVES: 8

400 g/14 oz walnuts

2 tbsp olive oil

25 g/1 oz butter

1.2 kg /2 lb 10 oz skinless, boneless chicken thighs

2 onions, thinly sliced

1 litre/1¾ pints hot chicken stock

300 ml/10 fl oz pomegranate molasses

1 tbsp dark brown sugar

1 pomegranate, seeds only

pinch of sea salt (optional)

pinch of pepper (optional)

4 tbsp finely chopped fresh coriander, to garnish

1. Preheat the oven to 180°C/350°F/Gas Mark 4. Put the walnuts on a baking tray in a single layer and roast for 8–10 minutes, or until golden brown, checking them often as they will burn easily. Leave them to cool completely, then finely grind them in a food processor. Reduce the oven temperature to 150°C/300°F/Gas Mark 2.

2. Heat half the oil and half the butter in a large frying pan over a high heat until hot. Working in batches, fry the chicken thighs for 6–8 minutes, or until golden brown, turning halfway through, then transfer to a plate. (You can use two frying pans to speed up this stage if you wish.) Add more butter and oil to the pan as needed.

3. Heat any remaining butter and oil, plus any cooking juices from the plate, in the pan over a medium heat until hot. Add the onions and fry, covered, for 10–15 minutes, or until softened and golden brown, stirring occasionally.

4. Tip the browned chicken and onions into a large casserole dish. Add the stock and bring to the boil. Reduce the heat to medium–low and, with the stock simmering, add the ground walnuts, pomegranate molasses and sugar. Stir well, then cover and bake for 2 hours, or until the sauce has darkened from beige to chocolatey brown and the chicken is cooked through and has fallen apart in big chunks.

5. Stir in half the pomegranate seeds and salt and pepper to taste, if using. Serve in bowls, scattered with the remaining pomegranate seeds and the coriander.

Cook's tip: *For extra richness, use 1.6 kg/3 lb 8 oz bone-in chicken thighs, but remove the bones, if you wish, before serving.*

Spiced Turkey Stew with Wholegrain Couscous

PREP: 20 minutes
COOK: 25 minutes
SERVES: 4

1 tbsp olive oil

500 g/1 lb 2 oz skinless, boneless
   turkey breast, cut into
   2-cm/¾-inch pieces

1 onion, roughly chopped

2 garlic cloves, finely chopped

1 red pepper, deseeded and
   roughly chopped

1 orange pepper, deseeded and
   roughly chopped

500 g/1 lb 2 oz tomatoes, roughly chopped

1 tsp cumin seeds, crushed

1 tsp paprika

grated zest and juice of 1 unwaxed lemon

pinch of sea salt

pinch of pepper

2 tbsp roughly chopped fresh flat-leaf
   parsley, to garnish

2 tbsp roughly chopped fresh coriander,
   to garnish

200 g/7 oz wholegrain giant couscous,
   to serve

Cumin and paprika combine with fresh herbs to give this Moroccan stew great depth of flavour.

1. Heat the oil in a large frying pan over a medium heat. Add the turkey, a few pieces at a time, then the onion, and fry for 5 minutes, or until golden brown, stirring often.

2. Stir in the garlic, red and orange peppers and tomatoes, then the cumin, paprika, lemon juice, salt and pepper. Cover and simmer for 20 minutes, or until the tomatoes have formed a thick sauce and the turkey is cooked through, stirring occasionally.

3. Meanwhile, half-fill a saucepan with water and bring to the boil. Add the couscous and cook according to the packet instructions, or until just tender. Tip into a sieve and drain well.

4. Spoon the couscous into shallow bowls and top with the stew. Mix the parsley and coriander with the lemon zest, then sprinkle over the stew and serve.

Cook's tip: *This is ideal if you are counting calories, as turkey is low-fat, especially if you remove the skin.*

This fragrant, golden, lemony chicken stew is the perfect pick-me-up for when you're feeling under the weather. It needs little accompaniment, although a bowl of steaming, buttery basmati rice is delicious with it.

Saffron, Chicken & Vegetable Stew

PREP: 25 minutes
COOK: 45 minutes
SERVES: 4

1 tbsp olive oil

25 g/1 oz butter

½ onion, finely chopped

2 garlic cloves, finely chopped

1 leek, thinly sliced

300 g/10½ oz carrots, finely chopped

pinch of saffron threads

100 ml/3½ fl oz boiling water

300 g/10½ oz skinless, boneless chicken thighs, halved

300 ml/10 fl oz hot chicken stock

175 g/6 oz baby leeks, halved lengthways

150 g/5½ oz baby carrots, halved lengthways

juice of 1 lemon

2 tbsp finely chopped fresh flat-leaf parsley

pinch of sea salt (optional)

pinch of pepper (optional)

1. Heat the oil and butter in a large saucepan over a medium heat until the butter stops foaming. Add the onion, garlic, thinly sliced leek and finely chopped carrots, reduce the heat to medium–low and cook for 10 minutes, covered, stirring occasionally.

2. Meanwhile, grind the saffron in a pestle and mortar, then add the boiling water, swirl and tip into a small bowl. Leave to steep.

3. Add the chicken, saffron water and stock to the cooked vegetables and bring to the boil. Reduce the heat to low and simmer, covered, for 20 minutes. Add the baby leeks and baby carrots and cook for a further 10 minutes, or until the chicken is cooked through.

4. Stir in the lemon juice and parsley and season with the salt and pepper to taste, if using, then serve.

Cook's tip: For extra flavour, use bone-in chicken thighs, removing the bones and shredding the chicken back into the stew in large chunks after cooking. Be aware the chicken takes longer to cook with the bone in.

This North African take on fish stew has a tomato base and is infused with spices and preserved lemon.

Moroccan Fish Tagine

PREP: 15 minutes
COOK: 1 hour 10 minutes
SERVES: 4

2 tbsp olive oil

1 large onion, finely chopped

pinch of saffron threads

½ tsp ground cinnamon

1 tsp ground coriander

½ tsp ground cumin

½ tsp ground turmeric

200 g/7 oz canned chopped tomatoes

300 ml/10 fl oz hot fish stock

4 small red mullet, scaled, filleted and pin-boned

55 g/2 oz stoned green olives

½ preserved lemon, rinsed and finely chopped

4 tbsp roughly chopped fresh coriander

2 pinches of sea salt

pinch of pepper

400 g/14 oz couscous, to serve

15 g/½ oz butter, to serve

1. Heat the oil in a large saucepan over a very low heat. Add the onion and cook for 10 minutes, or until softened but not coloured, stirring occasionally. Add the saffron, cinnamon, ground coriander, cumin and turmeric, and cook for 30 seconds, stirring constantly.

2. Add the tomatoes and stock, stir well and increase the heat to medium–high. Bring to the boil, then reduce the heat to medium–low, cover and simmer for 15 minutes. Uncover and simmer for a further 20–35 minutes, or until thickened.

3. Meanwhile, put the couscous in a shallow heatproof bowl. Add the butter and a pinch of salt. Pour over enough boiling water to cover by 2.5 cm/1 inch, place a folded tea towel over the top and set aside for 10 minutes, or until the couscous is tender and the liquid has been absorbed.

4. Cut each red mullet fillet in half, then push them into the tomato sauce. Simmer for 5–6 minutes, or until the fish is cooked.

5. Stir the olives, preserved lemon, 3 tablespoons of the fresh coriander and a pinch of salt and pepper into the tagine. Fluff up the couscous using a fork. Serve the tagine, garnished with the remaining fresh coriander, with the couscous.

Cook's tip: *Add a handful of raw peeled and deveined prawns (defrosted if frozen) to the tagine with the red mullet if you wish, and cook until they are pink. Garnish with a handful of toasted flaked almonds too, for an authentic Middle Eastern look.*

Meat in the Middle Eastern kitchen

Meat is enjoyed throughout the Middle East, slow-cooked with spices in rich tagines, quickly flame-grilled over charcoal as a street-side snack, or minced and blended for meltingly soft kebabs. For feasts or special occasions, a lamb might be spiced and roasted whole, stuffed with rice and raisins. For everyday cooking, inexpensive cuts of meat are used to flavour soups and stews, while mince is a popular filling for pies and pastries and more expensive cuts are cooked quickly, often as street food.

Lamb and mutton are eaten all over the region, whether grilled, simmered in stews, or roasted, although in many dishes beef can be substituted for lamb if you prefer. Mince is very common, as it's a thrifty way to use up fatty, cheaper cuts, such as beef or lamb neck, flank steak or scrag end of lamb. If you're making your own mince at home, be sure to use this type of cut, as the fat helps to prevent the meat from becoming dry when cooked. In Middle Eastern homes, mince is pounded repeatedly until it is very soft and almost paste-like. This gives very tender meatballs, kofte (pages 36 and 66) and kibbeh (page 18), which can be eaten by themselves or incorporated in miniature form into soups and stews. You can replicate this pounding process by using a food processor to further grind mince.

When they're not used for mince, cheaper cuts such as lamb neck and chuck steak are the perfect choice for slow-cooked tagines, biryanis or stews, as they'll fall apart beautifully after a long, slow cook over a low heat. Chicken tagines and stews should also be cooked on a very low heat to keep the meat from becoming tough, and again the best cuts are the cheaper thighs and drumsticks, with the bone in for additional flavour.

Offal is found in a wide variety of Middle Eastern dishes, with whole sheep's heads, stomachs and trotters cooked in broth, known as *pacha* in Iraq, and lamb brain, liver, heart, lungs, testicles and kidneys used for kebabs in Iran. Lamb or calf brains, often regarded as a delicacy, are eaten crumbed and fried, in salads or as a filling for small pies. In some regions, cooking fat is derived from rendered sheep's tail, known as *alya*, although olive oil or clarified butter are now more commonly used.

More expensive cuts of meat should be saved for quick-cook steaks or skewers. Traditionally, meat skewers are cooked as street food over charcoal braziers, but you can replicate the process at home under a hot grill or over a barbecue. Thread cubed beef fillet, sirloin, lamb loin or chicken breast onto skewers to make kebabs – the Middle East's most popular street food. You can find recipes for chicken kebabs on page 24 and beef kebabs on page 60.

Iranian Fish Stew

PREP: 30 minutes
COOK: 45 minutes
SERVES: 4

85 g/3 oz tamarind block

approx. 750 ml/1¼ pints boiling water

1 dried lime

1 tbsp olive oil

1 tsp fenugreek seeds

1 onion, finely chopped

3 garlic cloves, finely chopped

3 celery sticks, finely chopped

1 tbsp dark brown sugar

2 tbsp fresh or dried fenugreek leaves

60 g/2¼ oz fresh coriander, roughly
    chopped, plus 2 tbsp finely chopped
    to garnish

1 tbsp plain flour

1½ tsp ground turmeric

600 g/1 lb 5 oz firm-fleshed white fish,
    such as cod or hake, skinned, pin-boned
    and cut into 5-cm/2-inch pieces

2 tsp sea salt flakes

2 tbsp clarified butter

200 g/7 oz raw king prawns, peeled and
    deveined, defrosted if frozen

This herby fish stew, also known as *ghalieh mahi*, uses a sour-sweet combination of dried lime and tamarind that is popular in Iranian cooking. It is easy to cook and perfect with steamed basmati rice. You can find dried limes, whole tamarind blocks and fenugreek leaves in Middle Eastern shops.

1. Put the tamarind in a shallow heatproof bowl, add enough of the boiling water to cover, then leave for 20 minutes.

2. Meanwhile, grind the dried lime in a pestle and mortar. Heat the oil in a large saucepan over a low heat. Add the fenugreek seeds and fry for 2 minutes, or until aromatic. Add the onion and fry for 5 minutes, or until softened. Add the garlic, celery and crushed dried lime, cover and fry for 15 minutes, stirring occasionally.

3. Meanwhile, press the tamarind and its soaking water through a sieve into a measuring jug using the back of a spoon, pushing all the pulp through and leaving behind only the seeds and fibres. Scrape underneath the sieve using a clean spoon to get all the pulp. If necessary, top up with enough of the remaining boiling water to make up 750 ml/1¼ pints.

4. Stir the tamarind water, sugar, fenugreek leaves and half the coriander into the onion mixture. Bring to the boil, then reduce the heat to low and simmer, partly covered, for 15 minutes.

5. Meanwhile, mix together the flour and turmeric on a large plate. Dust the fish generously with this, then sprinkle with the salt.

6. Line a plate with kitchen paper. Heat the clarified butter in a large frying pan over a high heat. Working in batches, fry the floured fish for 2–3 minutes, or until golden brown, turning halfway through. Transfer to the prepared plate.

7. Add the fried fish, prawns and the remaining roughly chopped coriander to the stew. Bring to the boil, then reduce the heat to low and simmer very gently for 3 minutes, or until the prawns turn pink and the fish is cooked. Serve hot, scattered with the finely chopped coriander.

Cook's tip: *You can prepare the base of the stew in advance and store, covered, in the refrigerator for up to a day, then reheat it slowly on the hob and proceed from step five just before serving.*

Tagine takes its name from the earthenware pot in which it is traditionally slow-cooked over an open fire. Freekeh is toasted wheat and makes a delicious accompaniment.

Chicken Tagine with Freekeh

PREP: 30 minutes
COOK: 1 hour
SERVES: 4

1 tsp rose harissa

1 tbsp cumin seeds

½ tsp pepper

1 tsp sea salt flakes

125 ml/4 fl oz olive oil

1 kg/2 lb 4 oz mixed root vegetables, such as carrots, turnips and potatoes, cut into large chunks

8 skinless, boneless chicken thighs, about 150 g/5½ oz each

2 onions, roughly chopped

2 garlic cloves, thinly sliced

150 ml/5 fl oz hot chicken stock

225 g/8 oz freekeh, rinsed

750 ml/1¼ pints water

6 tbsp roughly chopped fresh coriander, to garnish

1. Whisk the rose harissa, cumin, pepper, half the salt and 5 tablespoons of the oil together in a jug. Put the root vegetables in a shallow dish, pour half the marinade over them and toss. Put the chicken in another shallow dish and pour the remaining marinade over it.

2. Heat 2 tablespoons of the remaining oil in a large heavy-based saucepan over a medium–low heat. Add the onions and fry for 5 minutes, or until softened. Add the garlic and fry for 2 minutes. Add the marinated vegetables, cover and cook for 10 minutes.

3. Meanwhile, heat the remaining oil in a frying pan over a medium–high heat. Add the chicken and cook for 6–8 minutes, until browned all over, turning occasionally. Transfer the chicken to the vegetables. Pour in the stock, cover and bring to the boil. Stir, then reduce the heat to low and simmer for 30 minutes, or until the chicken is cooked through.

4. Meanwhile, put the freekeh, water and remaining salt in a saucepan. Bring to the boil, then reduce the heat, cover and simmer for 25 minutes.

5. Tip the chicken and vegetables into a colander set over a large bowl. Pour the drained juices back into the frying pan and simmer for 5 minutes, or until thickened.

6. Drain the freekeh and tip it into a large serving dish. Arrange the chicken and vegetables on top and pour over the juices. Sprinkle with the coriander and serve immediately.

Cook's tip: *A tablespoon of finely chopped preserved lemons is a good addition with the stock before simmering in step three.*

Vegetable Tagine

PREP: 30 minutes
COOK: 40 minutes
SERVES: 4

2 tbsp olive oil

1 large onion, finely chopped

3 garlic cloves, crushed

1 tbsp ground coriander

2 tsp ground cumin

2 tsp ground ginger

¼ tsp dried red chilli flakes

large pinch of saffron threads

2 red peppers, deseeded and roughly
 chopped

250 g/9 oz peeled, deseeded
 and roughly chopped pumpkin or squash

400 g/14 oz canned chopped tomatoes

2 tbsp tomato purée

125 g/4½ oz ready-to-eat dried apricots,
 figs or prunes, roughly chopped

½ preserved lemon, rinsed and
 thinly sliced

1 bay leaf

30 g/1 oz fresh coriander, leaves and
 stalks separated, stalks tied together
 and lightly crushed, leaves chopped
 and reserved to garnish

3 pinches of sea salt

2 pinches of pepper

400 g/14 oz canned chickpeas in water,
 drained and rinsed

1 courgette, halved lengthways and sliced

55 g/2 oz baby spinach

1 tbsp toasted flaked almonds, to garnish

400 g/14 oz couscous, to serve

15 g/½ oz butter, to serve

Tagines can be made from almost any North African vegetable, but they must be prepared with classic flavourings such as preserved lemon, dried apricots, ginger, cumin and coriander, and then slow-cooked.

1. Heat the oil in a large heavy-based saucepan over a medium–high heat. Add the onion and fry for 3–4 minutes, or until softened, stirring occasionally. Add the garlic and fry for 1–2 minutes, or until softened. Stir in the ground coriander, cumin, ginger, chilli flakes and saffron, and fry for 30 seconds.

2. Add the red peppers, pumpkin, tomatoes, tomato purée, dried apricots, preserved lemon, bay leaf, fresh coriander stalks and enough water to cover by 7.5 cm/3 inches. Season with a pinch of salt and pepper. Cover and bring to the boil. Reduce the heat to low and simmer for 20 minutes.

3. Meanwhile, put the couscous in a shallow heatproof bowl. Add the butter and season with a pinch of salt. Pour over enough boiling water to cover by 2.5 cm/1 inch, place a folded tea towel over the top and set aside for 10 minutes, or until the couscous is tender and the liquid has been absorbed.

4. Stir the chickpeas and courgette into the tagine and simmer for 5–10 minutes, or until the vegetables are tender. Stir in the spinach and leave it to wilt, then season with a pinch of salt and pepper. Discard the bay leaf and coriander stalks.

5. Fluff up the couscous using a fork. Garnish the tagine with the almonds and coriander leaves. Serve the tagine with the couscous.

Cook's tip: Don't be afraid to change the vegetables according to what you like or have available. Aubergines work particularly well, chopped and added with the other vegetables in step two.

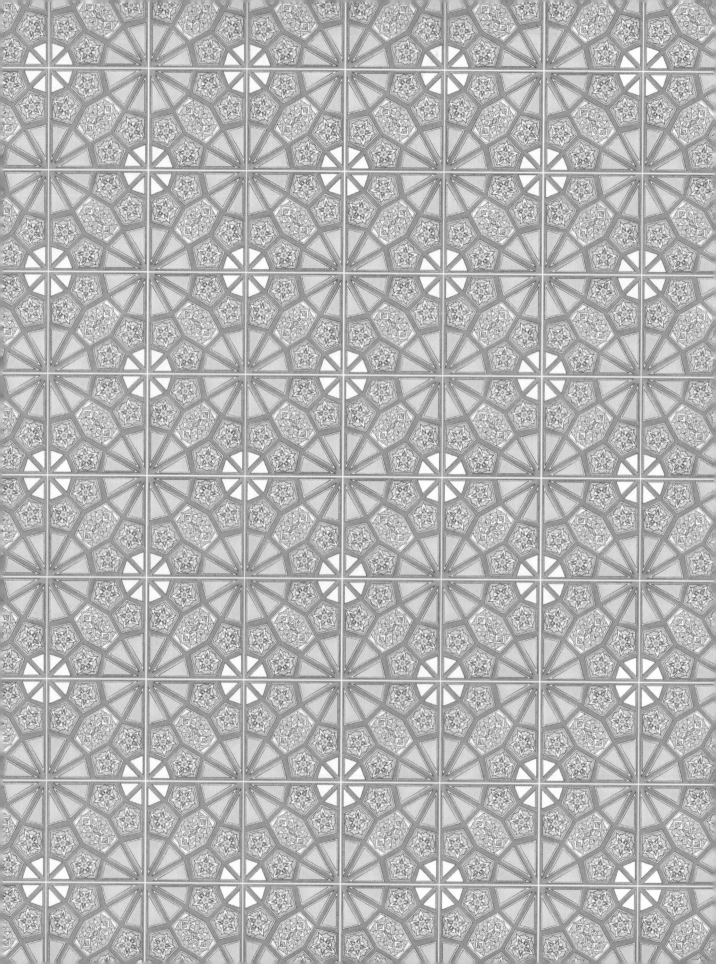

Grills & Roasts

Spicy Grilled Chicken Wraps

PREP: 20 minutes
MARINATE: 2 hours
COOK: 25 minutes
SERVES: 4

2 tsp fenugreek seeds

2 tsp fennel seeds

2 tsp cumin seeds

2 garlic cloves, finely chopped

pinch of freshly grated nutmeg

1 tsp cayenne pepper

grated zest and juice of 1 unwaxed lemon

1 tsp sea salt flakes, plus large pinch

2 tbsp Greek-style natural yogurt

4 skinless, boneless chicken breasts,
   about 175 g/6 oz each

2 tbsp olive oil

large pinch of pepper

To serve

8 wholemeal wraps

4 tbsp tahina sauce

2 tbsp rose harissa

2 tomatoes, roughly chopped

4 tbsp roughly chopped fresh coriander

This spiced grilled chicken is traditionally eaten for lunch or a light dinner.

1. Preheat a frying pan over a low heat until hot. Add the fenugreek, fennel and cumin, and toast for 2–3 minutes, or until aromatic. Leave to cool slightly, then crush in a pestle and mortar. Tip into a bowl, add the garlic, nutmeg, cayenne, lemon zest, 2 tablespoons of the lemon juice, 1 teaspoon of salt and the yogurt and mix well.

2. Slash the chicken all over using a sharp knife, then put it in a shallow non-reactive dish. Rub the marinade all over the chicken. Cover and marinate in the refrigerator for 2 hours.

3. To cook the chicken, preheat the grill to high. Line a baking tray with foil and place the marinated chicken on the tray. Drizzle it with the oil and sprinkle with a pinch of salt and pepper. Grill a few centimetres from the heat source for 20 minutes, or until cooked through, turning halfway through.

4. Leave the chicken to rest for a few minutes, then tear it into large shreds and serve with the wraps, tahina sauce, rose harissa, tomatoes and coriander, for your guests to make their own wraps.

Cook's tip: *To check the chicken is cooked through, pierce the thickest part with a skewer. Any juices that run out should be piping hot and clear with no traces of red or pink.*

Perfect for a barbecue, these spicy marinated beef shish skewers go well with Zhoug (page 162) and a heap of fluffy white rice or flatbreads. As they're only cooked briefly, under a very high heat, it's important to use a quick-cook steak such as sirloin. You will need 20 wooden skewers for this recipe.

Beef Shish Kebabs with Mushrooms, Red Onions & Peppers

PREP: 25 minutes
MARINATE: 2 hours
COOK: 15 minutes
MAKES: 20

juice of 1 lemon

2 tsp ground cumin

2 tsp ground coriander

2 tsp ground cinnamon

½ tsp cayenne pepper

2 garlic cloves, crushed

2 tbsp olive oil

600 g/1 lb 5 oz sirloin steak, trimmed of fat and cut into 2-cm/¾-inch cubes

200 g/7 oz button or chestnut mushrooms, halved or quartered if large

1 large red onion, cut into 2-cm/¾-inch chunks

1 red pepper, deseeded and cut into 2-cm/¾-inch chunks

1 tsp sea salt flakes

1 tbsp fresh coriander leaves, to garnish

1. Put the lemon juice, cumin, coriander, cinnamon, cayenne, garlic and oil in a large bowl and stir well. Add the steak, mushrooms, red onion and red pepper and mix well. Cover and marinate in the refrigerator for at least 2 hours, or overnight.

2. When you are ready to cook the kebabs, soak 20 wooden skewers in water for 20 minutes, then drain well. Preheat the oven to 230°C/450°F/Gas Mark 8. Line two baking trays with foil.

3. Thread the steak onto the skewers, alternating with the vegetables, and place them on the prepared baking trays. Sprinkle with the salt. Roast for 10 minutes for medium–rare or 12 minutes for medium, then cut into a steak cube to check it is done to your liking.

4. Leave the skewers to rest for 5 minutes under foil. Sprinkle with the fresh coriander and serve.

Cook's tip: If you like steak well done, increase the baking time in step three to 14–15 minutes. However, be aware that because the steak is cut so small it will be a lot tougher than well done steak usually is.

This dish takes minutes to prepare, and makes a delicious, easy midweek meal. The spicy, crunchy topping contrasts beautifully with the soft fish flakes.

Spiced Baked Cod with Harissa & Pine Nut Crust & Roast Cherry Tomatoes

PREP: 10 minutes
COOK: 15 minutes
SERVES: 2

30 g/1 oz pine nuts

15 g/½ oz fresh or dried white
  breadcrumbs

grated zest of 1 unwaxed lemon

2 tbsp roughly chopped fresh coriander

pinch of sea salt

1 tsp olive oil

200 g/7 oz cherry tomatoes on the vine

2 cod fillets, about 200 g/7 oz each

2 tsp rose harissa

1. Preheat the oven to 200°C/400°F/Gas Mark 6. Crush the pine nuts in a pestle and mortar. Tip them into a bowl, add the breadcrumbs, lemon zest, coriander, salt and oil and mix well.

2. Put the cherry tomatoes on a large baking tray and add the cod fillets skin side-down, arranging everything in a single layer. Spread a teaspoon of rose harissa over each cod fillet, then top with the breadcrumb mixture, pressing down gently.

3. Bake on a high shelf in the oven for 15 minutes, or until the topping is crisp and golden and the fish flakes easily when pressed with a knife. Serve the cod hot with the tomatoes.

Cook's tip: *Substitute the cod for pollack, coley or any other firm white fish – whatever is freshest and best value on the day.*

The full flavour of the lemony harissa dressing soaks into the steak, which unusually is marinated after cooking instead of before.

Chargrilled Steak with Harissa

PREP: 20 minutes
COOK: 8 minutes
MARINATE: 10 minutes
SERVES: 2

2 sirloin or rump steaks, about 2-cm/¾-inch thick

pinch of sea salt

pinch of pepper

2 tbsp olive oil

Harissa dressing

1 heaped tbsp rose harissa

4 tbsp roughly chopped fresh mint

grated zest and juice of 1 unwaxed lemon

3 tbsp extra virgin olive oil

pinch of sea salt

1. Season the steaks on both sides with the salt and pepper and rub them well with the olive oil. Set aside for 10 minutes.

2. For the dressing, whisk the rose harissa, mint, lemon zest and juice, extra virgin olive oil and salt together in a jug. Add more harissa if you prefer a spicier dressing. Pour the dressing into a non-reactive dish large enough to hold both steaks.

3. Heat a griddle pan or heavy-based frying pan over a high heat until smoking hot. Put the steaks in the pan, one at a time if they are large, and cook for 1½ minutes on each side for rare, 2 minutes for medium–rare and 3–4 minutes for well done. If your steak is thinner or thicker than 2 cm/¾ inch you'll need to adjust the cooking time.

4. Transfer the steaks to the dish containing the dressing and spoon it over them. Cover the dish with foil and leave to rest for 10 minutes.

5. Lift the steaks onto plates and slice each one. Tip the juices back into the dressing, whisk and spoon over the steaks.

Cook's tip: *Rump steak sits behind the sirloin and can offer good value; if you buy it from a butcher, ask for a cut from the upper end.*

These herby, spiced kofte are crisp on the outside and meltingly soft in the middle, with a hidden cube of feta cheese providing a salty kick. You can serve this as a main course with salads and flatbreads. You will need eight small wooden skewers for this recipe.

Lamb Kofte with Yogurt & Mint Dip

PREP: 30 minutes
CHILL: 1 hour
COOK: 30 minutes
MAKES: 8

1 onion, finely chopped

3 garlic cloves, finely chopped

25 g/1 oz fresh mint, finely chopped, plus extra leaves to garnish

4 tbsp finely chopped fresh coriander leaves and stalks

1 tsp ground cinnamon

1 tsp ground cumin

1 tsp ground ginger

2 tsp sea salt flakes

450 g/1 lb fresh lamb mince

75 g/2¾ oz feta cheese, cut into 8 cubes

2 tbsp olive oil

200 g/7 oz Greek-style natural yogurt, to serve

1. Put the onion and garlic on a chopping board and, using a sharp knife, mince them together into a paste (do not use a food processor or the mixture will get too wet). Transfer to a large bowl. Add 15 g/½ oz mint, all the coriander, cinnamon, cumin and ginger, and 1½ teaspoons of salt and stir. Using your hands, mix in the mince.

2. Divide the mixture into eight portions, then roll the first into a ball before flattening it on one palm. Place a cube of feta in the centre of the ball, then roll up the sides to enclose the cheese before patting the mixture into a flattened torpedo-shaped patty. Repeat with the remaining mixture and feta, then cover and refrigerate the kofte for at least 1 hour, or until firm.

3. Meanwhile, soak eight small wooden skewers in water for 20 minutes, then drain well. Preheat the oven to 180°C/350°F/Gas Mark 4.

4. For the dip, mix together the yogurt and remaining mint and salt in a bowl.

5. Heat a griddle pan or heavy-based frying pan over a high heat until smoking hot. Thread each kofte onto a skewer and brush them with a little oil. Cook for 6–8 minutes, or until crisp and a golden brown crust has formed, turning halfway through. Transfer to a baking tray and bake for 10 minutes, or until cooked through.

6. Serve the kofte hot, garnished with extra mint leaves, with the yogurt and mint dip.

Cook's tip: *To check the seasoning in the raw kofte mixture, break off a small piece and fry it until cooked, then taste and adjust the seasoning in the rest of the mixture.*

Turkey schnitzel is a popular Israeli dish. Here, spiced up with fragrant za'atar, it makes a satisfying dinner when served with a light salad. Try it in pitta breads for lunch.

Za'atar-spiced Turkey Schnitzel with Tahina Sauce

PREP: 20 minutes
COOK: 8 minutes
SERVES: 2

2 heaped tsp za'atar spice, plus 2 pinches

4 tbsp plain flour

3 pinches of sea salt flakes

55 g/2 oz dried breadcrumbs

1 egg

1 turkey breast, weighing 350 g/12 oz, or 2 portion-sized turkey breast fillets

4 tbsp olive oil

2 tbsp tahina sauce, to serve

½ lemon, cut into wedges, to serve

1. Mix 2 heaped teaspoons of za'atar, the flour and a pinch of salt on a large plate and set aside. Pour the breadcrumbs onto a separate plate. Crack the egg into a shallow bowl and whisk briefly.

2. If using a whole turkey breast, butterfly it, then cut through so you have two thin fillets.

3. Place the turkey fillets on a chopping board, spaced widely apart. Cover with clingfilm, then bash each fillet in turn using a rolling pin until it's less than 5 mm/¼ inch thick all over. It's important to do this properly, as it tenderizes the meat and makes it quick to cook.

4. Dip each turkey fillet first into the seasoned flour, then into the egg, then into the breadcrumbs.

5. Line a plate with kitchen paper. Heat 1 tablespoon of oil in a large frying pan over a medium–high heat. Fry the first schnitzel for 2 minutes on each side, adding another tablespoon of oil to the pan halfway through cooking. To check if the turkey is cooked, pierce the thickest part of the schnitzel with a skewer. Any juices should be piping hot and clear with no traces of red or pink. Transfer the schnitzel to the plate. Repeat with the second schnitzel.

6. Serve the schnitzels hot, each sprinkled with a pinch of salt and za'atar, with the tahina sauce and lemon wedges for squeezing over.

Cook's tip: *If you're scaling up the recipe to cook for more than two people, preheat your oven to 50°C/125°F or the lowest gas mark. Pop each cooked schnitzel on a baking tray and keep warm in the oven while you fry the remaining ones.*

This is a wonderful way to prepare whole fish. The spices aren't overpowering, but have just the right amount of heat and flavour to complement the fish and give it a crisp crust that contrasts with its soft flesh. The recipe is easily scaled up if you're cooking for more than two people. Serve with steamed vegetables or samphire.

Whole Spice-crusted Red Snapper

PREP: 10 minutes
COOK: 20 minutes
SERVES: 2

2 whole red snapper, scaled and gutted

grated zest of 1 unwaxed lemon, plus
  1 lemon, thinly sliced

3½ tbsp dukkah spice

60 g/2¼ oz ground almonds

4 tbsp olive oil

4 tbsp finely chopped fresh coriander

2 tsp sea salt flakes

1. Preheat the oven to 200°C/400°F/Gas Mark 6. Line a large roasting tin with baking paper and lay the fish on top.

2. Mix the lemon zest, dukkah spice, ground almonds, oil, coriander and salt together in a bowl.

3. Spoon 2 tablespoons of the mixture over one side of each fish, pressing it down gently to make a crust. Turn each fish over and spoon 2 tablespoons of the mixture on the other side. Put any remaining mixture in the cavities. Divide the lemon slices between the cavities.

4. Roast for 20 minutes, or until the fish flakes easily when pressed with a knife. Leave to rest for 2 minutes before serving hot.

Cook's tip: When buying whole fish, look for bright and clear eyes, shiny skin and bright-red gills and make sure it smells fresh. If the eyes are sunken and dull or it smells 'fishy', don't buy it. If you can't find red snapper, sea bream is also good for this dish.

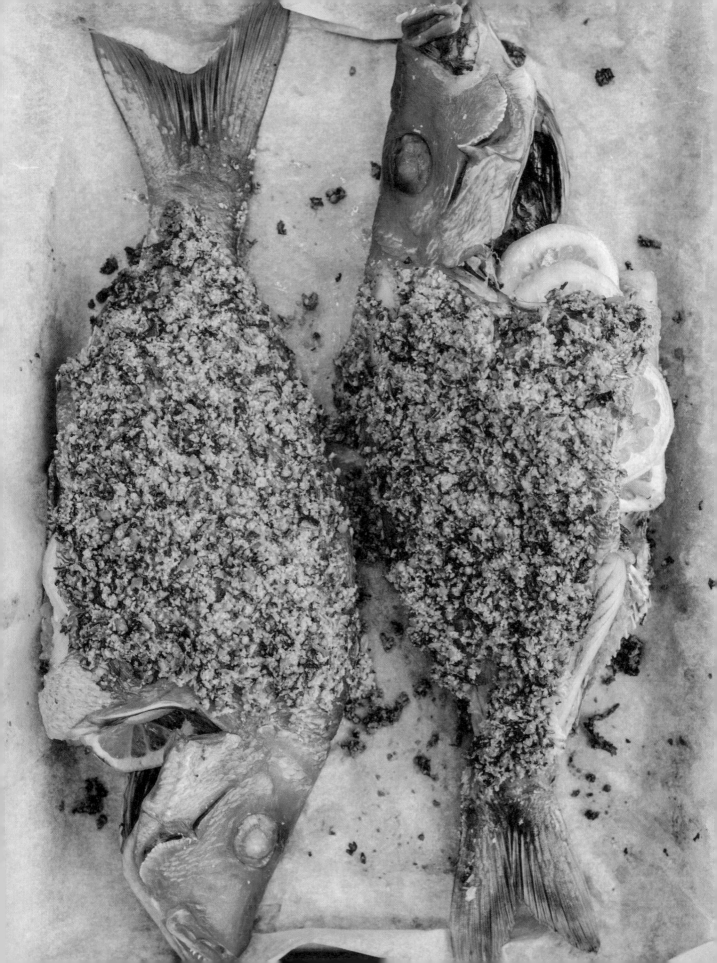

This combination of sweet and savoury ingredients is popular in the Middle East. Here, the delicately herby stuffing brings feta and pine nuts together with raisins and lemon. It complements the grilled sardines perfectly. You will need 24 cocktail sticks for this recipe.

Grilled Sardines Stuffed with Feta, Pine Nuts & Lemon

PREP: 30 minutes
COOK: 6 minutes
SERVES: 4

12 sardines, gutted and heads removed

100 g/3½ oz pine nuts

85 g/3 oz raisins

100 g/3½ oz feta cheese, crumbled

grated zest of 2 unwaxed lemons, plus 1 lemon, cut into wedges, to serve (optional)

40 g/1½ oz fresh flat-leaf parsley, finely chopped

pinch of sea salt

pinch of pepper

3 tbsp olive oil

1. Butterfly the sardines and remove the backbones (see Cook's tip, below).

2. Place a frying pan over a low heat until hot. Add the pine nuts and toast for 5–6 minutes, or until golden, tossing halfway through. Leave to cool, then grind half the nuts in a pestle and mortar. Transfer them to a bowl, add the raisins, feta, lemon zest, parsley, whole pine nuts, salt and pepper, and mix well.

3. Spoon 2 teaspoons of the filling into the cavity of each butterflied sardine. Close each sardine like a book and secure using a couple of cocktail sticks or a piece of string.

4. Preheat the grill to high. Line a baking tray with foil. Lay the filled sardines on the prepared tray and drizzle over half the oil. Grill for 6 minutes, turning halfway through and drizzling with the remaining oil. Serve hot, with lemon wedges for squeezing over, if using.

Cook's tip: *To butterfly a sardine, open out the gutted fish and lay it skin side-up on your work surface. Hold the tail with one hand and firmly press along the backbone with the other until the fish is flat. Remove the head if this has not been done already. Turn the fish over and gently pull away the backbone, then cut it out. Remove any remaining small bones using tweezers.*

Moroccan-spiced Roast Chicken with Stuffed Onions

PREP: 20 minutes
MARINATE: 2 hours
COOK: 1½ hours
SERVES: 6

5 garlic cloves

3 tbsp Greek-style natural yogurt, plus 3 tbsp to serve (optional)

1 tsp ground cumin

1 tsp ground coriander

2 tsp cayenne pepper

½ tsp ground turmeric

2 tsp sea salt flakes, plus 2 pinches

2 tsp ground ginger

2.5-cm/1-inch piece of fresh ginger, peeled and finely grated

1 lemon, halved, plus grated zest of 1 unwaxed lemon

1 ready-to-cook chicken, weighing 2 kg/4 lb 8 oz

8 small red onions, peeled

75 g/2¾ oz butter, softened

1 tbsp sumac spice

6 tbsp finely chopped fresh mint

pinch of pepper

This roast chicken is a great centrepiece for a special Sunday lunch with friends. Marinating the chicken for a few hours in the spice rub before roasting it improves its flavour and texture.

1. Grate two garlic cloves into a bowl. Add the yogurt, cumin, coriander, cayenne, turmeric, 2 teaspoons of the salt and the ground and fresh ginger. Squeeze in the juice of half a lemon and mix well.

2. Put the chicken in a large roasting tin and rub the spice mixture all over the skin and inside the cavity. Put the remaining garlic cloves and lemon half inside the chicken. Cover with clingfilm and marinate in the refrigerator for 2 hours.

3. When you are ready to cook, preheat the oven to 200°C/400°F/ Gas Mark 6. Cut a deep cross almost all the way through each onion. Put the butter, lemon zest, sumac, mint and a pinch of salt in a bowl and mix well. Stuff each onion with the butter mixture, then place them alongside the chicken. Roast for 1½ hours, or until cooked through. To check if the chicken is cooked, pierce the thickest part of the thigh with a skewer. Any juices should be piping hot and clear with no traces of red or pink. If the chicken is not cooked, return it to the oven for a further 10 minutes and check again.

4. Transfer the chicken and onions to a serving platter, cover loosely with foil and leave to rest for 10 minutes. Meanwhile, put the roasting tin over a medium heat and skim any excess fat off the liquid. Bring to the boil and reduce by half. Season with a pinch of salt and pepper, then stir in the remaining yogurt, if using. Serve the chicken and onions with the gravy.

Cook's tip: *To further check that a whole chicken is cooked, gently pull the leg away from the body. It should 'give' and no traces of pinkness or blood should remain.*

Griddled
Aubergine with
Pomegranate,
Coriander
& Yogurt
page 78

This dish is perfect for a grazing dinner, and can be easily scaled up if you're cooking for more than four people. You will need a piece of muslin for this recipe.

Griddled Aubergine with Pomegranate, Coriander & Yogurt

PREP: 15 minutes
COOK: 45 minutes
SERVES: 4 as a side dish, 2 as a main

300 g/10½ oz Greek-style natural yogurt

½ tsp sea salt flakes, plus a pinch

1 aubergine, cut into 5-mm/¼-inch slices

½ tsp ground turmeric

2 tbsp olive oil

3 tbsp finely chopped fresh coriander

½ pomegranate, seeds only

1. Line a sieve with muslin and set it over a bowl. Mix the yogurt and a pinch of salt together in a separate bowl, then place it in the prepared sieve. Bring the edges of the cloth up and gently twist them together, then leave to drain for 30 minutes. Discard the liquid.

2. Sprinkle the cut sides of each aubergine slice with the turmeric and salt and rub it in well.

3. Heat a griddle pan or heavy-based saucepan over a medium–high heat until smoking hot. Working in batches, brush one side of the aubergine slices with oil and place them on the griddle pan, oil side-down, pressing down gently. Cook for 3 minutes, then brush the tops with oil, flip them over and cook the other side for a further 3 minutes.

4. Place the aubergine on a large serving platter, in a single layer if possible. Leave to cool, then spread each with 2 teaspoons of the drained yogurt. Sprinkle with the coriander and pomegranate seeds. Serve at room temperature.

› **Pictured on previous page**

Cook's tip: This dish improves in flavour if kept in the refrigerator for a few hours. Allow to come back up to room temperature before serving.

This one-dish chicken recipe is rich with the Middle Eastern flavours of harissa and rosewater. It's simple enough for a midweek meal, but special enough for guests.

Roast Chicken Pieces with Harissa & Rosewater

PREP: 25 minutes
MARINATE: 1 hour
COOK: 1 hour 15 minutes
SERVES: 4

6 bone-in chicken thighs

6 bone-in chicken drumsticks

1 lemon, cut into 8 wedges

30 g/1 oz flaked almonds, to garnish

3 tbsp roughly chopped fresh coriander, to garnish

Marinade

1 tbsp olive oil

2 tbsp rose harissa

1 tsp rosewater

1 heaped tsp Greek-style natural yogurt

2 preserved lemons, rinsed and finely chopped

pinch of sea salt

1 tbsp rose petals (optional)

1. For the marinade, mix all the ingredients together in a bowl.

2. Using a sharp knife, make several deep slashes in each chicken piece. Rub the marinade into the chicken and put it in a shallow dish. Cover and marinate in the refrigerator for at least 1 hour, or overnight.

3. When you are ready to cook, preheat the oven to 180°C/350°C/ Gas Mark 4. Arrange the chicken and lemon in a single layer in a large roasting tin. Roast for 30 minutes, then increase the heat to 200°C/400°F/Gas Mark 6 and roast for a further 30–40 minutes, or until deep golden brown and cooked through. Push a skewer into the thickest part of a chicken piece; the meat should no longer be pink and the juices should be clear and piping hot. Cover the chicken with foil and leave to rest for 10 minutes.

4. Meanwhile, put the flaked almonds on a baking tray in a single layer and roast for 3–4 minutes, or until golden brown, checking them regularly as they will easily burn.

5. Scatter the chicken with the coriander and toasted almonds and serve.

> **Pictured overleaf**

Cook's tip: *Rosewater comes in different strengths, so taste your marinade to ensure you are happy with the flavour before using it.*

Roast
Chicken
Pieces with
Harissa &
Rosewater
page 79

Slow-roasting this spiced leg of lamb will give you meltingly tender meat, and will fill your kitchen with wonderful aromas. This dish creates its own delicious ras el hanout-flavoured gravy, but the Zhoug on page 162 is also an excellent accompaniment to cut through the richness of the lamb. If you're not cooking for six to eight, consider using a 1 kg/2 lb 4 oz half-leg of lamb, scaling the recipe down by half and roasting the lamb for a total of 3 hours instead of 3½ in step three – it's too delicious not to serve as a regular weekend lunch.

Ras el Hanout, Garlic & Thyme Roast Leg of Lamb

PREP: 15 minutes
COOK: 3½ hours
REST: 30 minutes
SERVES: 6–8

20 fresh lemon thyme sprigs

8 garlic cloves, peeled, plus 2 heads garlic, halved horizontally

4 tsp sea salt flakes, plus a pinch

4 tbsp ras el hanout

4 tbsp olive oil

1 leg of lamb, weighing 2–2.5 kg/4 lb 8 oz–5 lb 8 oz

2 onions, cut into quarters

300 ml/10 fl oz water

pinch of pepper, to serve

1 tbsp Greek-style natural yogurt, to serve

1. Preheat the oven to 150°C/300°F/Gas Mark 2. Strip the leaves from half the lemon thyme and put them in a pestle and mortar. Add the garlic cloves and 3 teaspoons of the salt and crush. Add the ras el hanout and oil, and mix to form a rough paste.

2. Put the lamb in a roasting tin. Using a sharp knife, make several small slits in the skin. Rub in the spice paste, working it into the slits well. Sprinkle over 1 teaspoon of salt, put the halved heads of garlic and quartered onions alongside it, sprinkle over the remaining lemon thyme, then pour the water around it.

3. Roast for 30 minutes, uncovered. Baste the lamb with the cooking liquid and cover the tray with foil. Roast for a further 3 hours, basting every half an hour.

4. Transfer the lamb to a serving platter, add the onions and garlic and leave to rest, covered in foil, for 30 minutes.

5. For the gravy, skim the excess oil off the liquid and season with a pinch of salt and pepper. Stir the yogurt into the gravy and serve alongside the roast lamb and onions.

Cook's tip: For a more intense gravy, after skimming off the oil in step five, tip the liquid from the roasting tin into a small saucepan and reduce it by half before checking for seasoning and stirring through the yogurt off the heat.

This spiced salmon makes a quick and easy midweek dinner, but tastes spectacular enough for guests too. Cooking salmon with pomegranate *en papillote* (in a parcel) gives the fish a wonderful sharpness and sweetness. This goes well with Freekeh, Broad Bean & Pea Salad with Dill & Pomegranate (page 132).

Roast Salmon with Spices, Pomegranate & Coriander

PREP: 10 minutes
COOK: 15–20 minutes
SERVES: 4

4 salmon fillets

2 tsp ras el hanout

1 tsp sea salt flakes

grated zest and juice of 1 unwaxed lemon

2 tsp olive oil

½ pomegranate, seeds only

4 tbsp roughly chopped fresh coriander

1. Preheat the oven to 180°C/350°F/Gas Mark 4. Cut out four rectangles of baking paper, each large enough to comfortably wrap a salmon fillet, and four slightly larger rectangles of foil. Lay each rectangle of baking paper over a rectangle of foil. Put a salmon fillet in the centre of each baking paper piece.

2. Sprinkle the fillets with the ras el hanout, salt, lemon zest and juice and oil, then the pomegranate seeds and coriander. Bring the long edges of the baking paper up together, before folding them down a few times to form a crisp pleat over the top of the salmon and tucking the short edges below. Repeat with the foil underneath to form a secure parcel.

3. Put the parcels on a baking tray. Roast on a high shelf of the oven for 15–20 minutes, or until the fish is cooked through and flakes easily when pressed with a knife. Serve the parcels for people to unwrap at the table.

Cook's tip: *Cooking fish in a parcel is ideal if you are cooking for one, as it is low on mess and high on flavour.*

Rice &
Vegetables

Persian Jewelled Rice

PREP: 20 minutes
SOAK: 1 hour
COOK: 35 minutes
SERVES: 4

400 g/14 oz basmati rice

1 tbsp full-fat milk

large pinch of saffron threads

4 tbsp clarified butter
  (shop-bought or see Cook's tip)

1 black cardamom pod

8 cloves

1 cinnamon stick

1 bay leaf

100 g/3½ oz whole blanched almonds

100 g/3½ oz unsalted pistachio nuts

1 large onion, thinly sliced

2 large pinches of sea salt

zest of 1 orange, finely pared and cut
  into thin strips

75 g/2¾ oz barberries or dried cranberries

750 ml/1¼ pints water

This traditional Persian rice is a festival dish – something to cook for a special occasion or when you've got friends around. It is known as 'jewelled' as the almonds represent pearls, the pistachios emeralds, the saffron and orange gold and the barberries rubies.

1. Rinse the rice in several changes of water, then soak it for 1 hour (if time permits).

2. Meanwhile, warm the milk in a small saucepan. Remove from the heat, add the saffron and leave to steep while you prepare the onions and nuts.

3. Heat 3 tablespoons of the clarified butter in a large saucepan over a low heat. Add the cardamom, cloves, cinnamon and bay leaf and fry for 1 minute, or until aromatic. Add the almonds and pistachio nuts and fry for 3–4 minutes, or until golden, tossing halfway through.

4. Transfer the spiced nuts to a plate using a slotted spoon. Increase the heat to medium, then add the onion and a large pinch of salt to the pan and fry for 10 minutes, or until golden and crisp, stirring occasionally. Add the final tablespoon of butter if the pan looks dry.

5. Drain the rice well, then stir it into the onion mixture. Add most of the orange zest and all the barberries and return the nut mixture to the pan. Fry for 3–4 minutes, stirring constantly.

6. Using the back of a teaspoon, press the saffron into the hot milk to release more colour, then tip it into the rice and onion mixture. Add a large pinch of salt and the water. Bring to the boil, stir well, then place a tight-fitting lid on the rice and turn the heat down to minimum. Cook for 15 minutes without lifting the lid.

7. Remove the lid, fluff up the rice using a fork, then tip it out onto a couple of large plates to steam dry. Serve hot, garnished with the remaining orange zest.

Cook's tip: To make 4 tablespoons of clarified butter, melt 85 g/3 oz unsalted butter in a small saucepan over a medium–low heat until it starts to crackle and foam. Line a sieve with muslin or a clean kitchen cloth and set it over a bowl. Pour the butter through the lined sieve. The bright yellow melted butter in the bowl is now clarified and can be heated to a high temperature without burning, as the milk solids that usually burn have been collected in the sieve.

The crisp, crunchy golden base or *tahdig* of Persian rice is delicious. Here, it is complemented by the sunshine yellow colour of the saffron rice – hence 'double golden'. You will need a large saucepan with a tight-fitting lid.

Double Golden Roast Saffron Rice

PREP: 10 minutes
COOK: 50 minutes
SERVES: 4

300 g/10½ oz basmati rice

large pinch of saffron threads

2 tsp boiling water

50 g/1¾ oz butter

1 tbsp extra virgin olive oil

large pinch of sea salt

1. Rinse the rice in several changes of cold water. Tip it into a saucepan and cover with five to six times its volume of boiling water. Parboil at a rolling boil for 5 minutes, stirring occasionally, then drain well.

2. Meanwhile, grind the saffron in a pestle and mortar. Add the boiling water, swirl and tip into a small bowl. Leave to steep.

3. Tip the rice into a large bowl. Mix in the saffron water until the rice is evenly golden.

4. Heat the butter, oil and salt in a large heavy-based saucepan over a medium heat until the butter stops sizzling. Spread a layer of rice over the base of the pan, then pile up the rest of the rice in a cone shape on top – this will help it to steam. Cover the pan with foil, then a lid, and clamp the foil down well over the sides. Cook for 5 minutes, or until the base becomes crispy, then reduce the heat to its lowest setting and cook for 40 minutes.

5. Remove from the heat and let the rice sit, covered, for 5 minutes. Remove the foil and lid and spoon the rice onto plates. Use a spatula to carefully lift the crispy rice from the bottom of the pan, and serve it on top of the rest of the rice.

Cook's tips: When mixing the saffron into the rice, tip a little rice into both the mortar and the small bowl the saffron has steeped in to get every last drop of saffron water. To allow as little steam as possible to escape from the rice, carefully wrap a folded clean tea towel over the foil and lid around the rim of the pan, but keep it well away from the hob, particularly if using a gas flame.

Lamb Biryani with Dried Apricots

PREP: 45 minutes
COOK: 3 hours
SERVES: 6

6 tbsp clarified butter

3 onions, half very thinly sliced
    and half finely chopped

3 pinches of sea salt

450 g/1 lb lamb neck, cut into cubes

1 tbsp olive oil (optional)

1 cinnamon stick

2 bay leaves

8 cloves

3 black cardamom pods

10 green cardamom pods, crushed

2 tsp ground ginger

2 tsp ground cumin

1 tsp ground coriander

½ tsp ground turmeric

200 g/7 oz ready-to-eat dried
    apricots, halved

400 ml/14 fl oz water

large pinch of saffron threads

2 tbsp full-fat milk

425 g/15 oz basmati rice

about 2 litres/3½ pints boiling water

150 g/5½ oz Greek-style natural yogurt

*Cook's tip: To rinse basmati rice
well, put it in a deep bowl and cover
it with plenty of cold water. Swirl
the rice, then tip out the water before
repeating three or four times. You've
washed most of the starch off when
the water runs clear as you swirl.*

This luxurious Persian festival dish is perfect for a party. It
takes a while to prepare, but you can cook the lamb a day
ahead and finish with the rice the next day if you prefer. It
goes well with Greek-style natural yogurt and Pomegranate
Salad with Herbs & Pistachios (page 142).

1. Preheat the oven to 150°C/300°F/Gas Mark 2. Heat 2 tablespoons
of the clarified butter in a large frying pan over a medium heat.
Add the sliced onions and a pinch of salt and fry for 10 minutes, or
until golden and crispy, stirring occasionally. Transfer the onions
to a plate using a slotted spoon. Using the same pan and working in
batches, brown the lamb for 2 minutes per side, then transfer to a
plate using a slotted spoon. Add oil between batches if needed.

2. Meanwhile, heat 2 tablespoons of the clarified butter in a large
casserole over a low heat. Add the cinnamon, bay, cloves and black
and green cardamom and cook for 1–2 minutes, or until aromatic.
Add the finely chopped onions and a large pinch of salt, then cover
and cook for 10 minutes, or until softened, stirring occasionally. Stir
in the ginger, cumin, coriander and turmeric and fry for 2 minutes.
Stir in the lamb and dried apricots, then remove from the heat.

3. Return the frying pan to the heat until hot. Pour in 100 ml/
3½ fl oz of the water and let it bubble for a few minutes, scraping up
all the flavour using a wooden spoon. Tip this into the spiced lamb.
Add the remaining water and bring to the boil. Reduce the heat to
low, cover with foil and a lid, then transfer to the oven to bake for
1½ hours. Leave to cool.

4. Grind the saffron in a pestle and mortar. Warm the milk in a small
saucepan. Remove from the heat, add the saffron and leave to steep.

5 Rinse the rice in several changes of cold water (see Cook's tip).
Tip it into a large saucepan and pour in the boiling water. Parboil
for 5 minutes, stirring occasionally, then drain well.

6. Stir the yogurt into the cooled lamb. Cover the base of a large
casserole dish with a few tablespoons of the sauce. Add a layer of
the parboiled rice, sprinkle with a few teaspoons of the saffron milk
and a pinch of salt, and top with some crispy onions and a layer of
lamb. Repeat these layers until you've used up all the rice, lamb and
onions, finishing with a layer of rice and saffron milk. Sprinkle with
the remaining clarified butter, cover with foil and put the lid on.
Cook on a medium heat for 5 minutes, then transfer to the oven and
bake for 40 minutes. Serve.

Iraqi Kitchree

PREP: 25 minutes
COOK: 50 minutes
SERVES: 6

200 g/7 oz basmati rice

200 g/7 oz red lentils

2 tbsp vegetable oil

2 tsp cumin seeds

2 onions, thinly sliced

3 large pinches of sea salt flakes

1 tsp ground turmeric

2 tsp ground cumin

2 tsp ground coriander

2 tsp ground ginger

600 ml/1 pint water

150 g/5 oz fresh podded
    or frozen peas (optional)

4 tbsp roughly chopped fresh coriander

2 large pinches of pepper

To serve

½ tbsp olive oil

6 eggs

300 g/10½ oz Greek-style natural
    yogurt (optional)

Kitchree is the original dish behind the popular Anglicized 'kedgeree'. It exists under various names and forms throughout the Middle East and India. It's made of things that households in the region usually have handy: rice, lentils and onions. While every region has its own variation, this Iraqi version is topped with a fried egg, which complements the soft-cooked rice and lentils perfectly.

1. Rinse the rice and red lentils in several changes of cold water.

2. Heat the vegetable oil in a large frying pan over a low heat. Add the cumin seeds and fry for 1 minute, or until aromatic. Add the onions, increase the heat to medium–high and fry for 10 minutes, or until golden brown and crispy. Transfer half the spiced onions to a plate and season with a large pinch of salt.

3. Add the turmeric, ground cumin, ground coriander, ginger and a large pinch of salt to the remaining onions in the frying pan and fry for 2 minutes, stirring often. Add the rice and lentils and fry for 2–3 minutes more. Tip the mixture into a large saucepan.

4. Pour the water into the saucepan and bring to the boil. Stir, reduce the heat to medium–low, cover and simmer for 30 minutes.

5. Blanch the peas, if using, in boiling water, then stir them and most of the fresh coriander into the *kitchree*. Season with the remaining salt and a pinch of pepper, adding extra water to loosen the texture if required.

6. To serve, heat the olive oil in a frying pan. Fry the eggs for 3 minutes, or until cooked to your liking (see Cook's tip). Pile the *kitchree* into six shallow bowls, then top with the yogurt, if using, a portion of the reserved fried onions, a fried egg and the remaining fresh coriander. Season with a large pinch of pepper.

Cook's tip: *Fry eggs for 3 minutes for a runny yolk. If you prefer a firmer yolk, add another minute or two to the cooking time.*

Mushroom & Aubergine Moussaka

PREP: 40 minutes
COOK: 1½ hours
SERVES: 6

3 large aubergines, thinly
 sliced lengthways

3 tbsp olive oil

1 tsp sea salt flakes, plus 3 pinches

Mushroom sauce

2 tbsp olive oil

2 onions, finely chopped

2 garlic cloves, finely chopped

600 g/1 lb 5 oz mixed chestnut and
 Portobello mushrooms, finely chopped

5 fresh sage leaves, finely chopped

5 sprigs fresh thyme, leaves only

2 sprigs fresh oregano, leaves finely
 chopped

½ tsp ground cinnamon

800 g/1 lb 12 oz canned chopped tomatoes

100 ml/3½ fl oz water

3 large pinches of pepper

Béchamel sauce

500 ml/17 fl oz full-fat milk

30 g/1 oz butter

40 g/1½ oz plain flour

pinch of freshly grated nutmeg

2 pinches of white pepper

40 g/1½ oz pecorino
 or Parmesan cheese, finely grated

1 egg, lightly beaten

This comforting Turkish dish is a perfect centrepiece to a vegetarian feast, with rich layers of silky aubergines, creamy béchamel and herby mushroom sauce. Fresh sage, thyme and oregano, used to flavour the mushrooms, are all popular in the Middle East. Traditionally, the aubergine slices are fried in hot oil, but this recipe saves time, effort and calories by roasting them instead.

1. Preheat the oven to 200°C/400°F/Gas Mark 6. Line two baking trays with baking paper. Lay the aubergine slices on the prepared trays, brush them on both sides with the oil and sprinkle with 1 teaspoon of the salt. Roast for 20 minutes, or until softened. Repeat if necessary until all the slices are cooked.

2. Meanwhile, for the mushroom sauce, heat the oil in a large frying pan over a low heat. Add the onions and garlic and fry for 10 minutes, or until softened, stirring often. Stir in the mushrooms and fry for 5 minutes. Stir in the sage, thyme, oregano and cinnamon and fry for 2 minutes. Add the tomatoes, water and a pinch of salt and pepper. Bring to the boil, then reduce the heat to medium–low and simmer, partially covered, for 20 minutes.

3. For the béchamel sauce, heat the milk in a milk pan until just below boiling point. Meanwhile, heat the butter in a saucepan over a medium–low heat until it starts to foam. Add the flour to the butter and stir constantly for 2 minutes, until you have a smooth mixture that comes away cleanly from the sides of the pan. Pour in the hot milk, a little at a time, stirring well between each addition to avoid lumps forming, until you have a thick, smooth sauce.

4. Increase the heat to medium–high and bring the béchamel to the boil, stirring constantly. Cook for 3 minutes, then stir in the nutmeg and white pepper. Remove from the heat and stir in the cheese and a pinch of salt and black pepper. Leave to cool, then whisk in the egg.

5. To assemble the moussaka, put a layer of aubergine in the base of a lasagne dish, spread a third of the mushroom sauce on top, then add another layer of aubergine and a further third of the mushroom sauce. Repeat with a final layer of both. Spread the béchamel evenly over the top, then season with the remaining salt and pepper.

6. Bake for 30–35 minutes, or until golden and puffed up. Leave to cool for 10–15 minutes before serving.

Spices in the Middle Eastern Kitchen

The best way to understand the variety of spices available to the Middle Eastern cook is to visit one of the region's souks or bazaars. Imagine yourself in the souk, surrounded by baskets of heaped spices. Many will be familiar to you – star anise, allspice berries, cinnamon sticks, cardamom pods, cloves, nutmeg, dried chillies and peppercorns, or caraway, coriander, cumin, fennel and fenugreek seeds – all piled up in glorious, headily aromatic abundance. It's a far cry from the tiny, uniform glass jars you find in the spice aisle of your local supermarket. When you buy these spices at home, it's always best to choose the whole spice, as you would at the souk, and grind them in small quantities as needed; that way they'll stay fresh and aromatic. Save time by using an electric coffee grinder for this, though a pestle and mortar is of course the traditional method.

More unusual spices at the souk include baskets of whole turmeric, which looks like fresh ginger, but smaller and bright yellow, as well as heaps of fenugreek leaves, sumac, cassia bark and dried chamomile. Prettiest of all are the piles of pink, jewel-like rosebuds, which are used in pilafs, chicken dishes and sweets. Behind the counter, you'll find highly prized and expensive Iranian saffron, used throughout the region for special occasions and festival cooking. Make saffron go a little further at home by pounding a small pinch with sea salt flakes in a pestle and mortar and storing the delicately coloured salt in a salt shaker, to finish off dishes with a burst of saffron flavour.

You'll also find many specialist regional ingredients at the spice souk, including heaps of musty grey-green dried limes, piled in mounds like hollow, misshapen golf balls. In hot countries, you can dry your own limes in the sun. Both dried limes and tamarind are used to give a distinctive and delicious sour flavour to Iranian and Iraqi cooking. In Moroccan cooking, preserved lemons are used for a similar purpose; try the recipe on page 166, as they're very easy to make.

All the spice shops in the souk sell similar whole spices, but what really sets them apart are the house blends on offer. The best blend will be ras el hanout – anything between 12 and 100 of the finest spices in the shop, made to a closely guarded secret recipe. Other popular blends, which you can now find in many supermarkets, include za'atar (dried thyme, salt and toasted sesame seeds) and dukkah (pounded cumin seeds, hazelnuts, sesame seeds and coriander seeds), both of which are popular mixed with olive oil as a dip for pitta breads. More specialist blends include Egyptian *quatre-épice* (pepper, nutmeg, cloves and cinnamon), Lebanese seven-spice (nutmeg, ginger, allspice, ground coriander, cloves, cinnamon and black pepper), or the pungent *baharat* (which may include coriander seeds, black pepper, cloves, cardamom, cumin seeds, cinnamon, sweet paprika, nutmeg, sumac, saffron, turmeric and chillies).

This summery salad tastes best served immediately, with the halloumi still hot from the pan. It can also be prepared a few hours in advance and stored in the refrigerator, then brought back to room temperature before serving. It's best eaten the day it's made, as the halloumi tends to lose its flavour if it sits in a salad for too long.

Chickpea, Halloumi, Red Onion & Coriander Salad

PREP: 10 minutes
COOK: 12 minutes
SERVES: 4

200 g/7 oz halloumi, sliced

400 g/14 oz canned chickpeas in water, drained and rinsed

1 red onion, finely chopped

3 tbsp finely chopped fresh coriander

juice of 1½ lemons

1 tbsp extra virgin olive oil

pinch of sea salt (optional)

pinch of pepper (optional)

1. Heat a griddle pan or heavy-based frying pan over a high heat until smoking hot. Working in batches, fry the halloumi in the dry pan for 4–6 minutes, or until charred, golden and crispy in places, turning halfway through. Transfer to a chopping board and leave to cool slightly, then cut into 1-cm/½-inch cubes.

2. Mix the halloumi, chickpeas, red onion, coriander, lemon juice and oil together in a large salad bowl. Mix in the salt and pepper, if using, then serve immediately.

Cook's tip: *Try this salad with Classic Tabbouleh (page 120).*

This North African breakfast of eggs baked in fiery spiced peppers, tomatoes, onions and garlic is popular throughout the Middle East. Serve it as a breakfast, or with a pile of flatbreads as a light dinner.

Shakshouka

PREP: 20 minutes
COOK: 45 minutes
SERVES: 4

3 tbsp olive oil

1 tsp cumin seeds

2 red onions, thinly sliced

2 garlic cloves, finely chopped

1 red chilli, deseeded and
  finely chopped

1 tsp sea salt flakes, plus a pinch

2 red peppers, deseeded and thinly sliced

3 vine tomatoes, roughly chopped

2 pinches of pepper

4 eggs

2 tsp za'atar spice

1. Preheat the oven to 180°C/350°F/Gas Mark 4. Heat the oil in a large ovenproof frying pan over a low heat. Add the cumin and fry for 1–2 minutes, or until aromatic. Add the red onions, garlic, chilli and 1 teaspoon of salt and fry for 5 minutes, or until softened, stirring often.

2. Add the red peppers and increase the heat to medium. Fry for 1 minute, stirring constantly. Reduce the heat to low, cover and cook for a further 20 minutes, stirring occasionally.

3. Add the tomatoes and a pinch of salt and pepper and cook for 5 minutes.

4. Using a wooden spoon, make four deep egg-sized indentations in the sauce, then crack an egg into each one. Sprinkle the za'atar over the eggs and sauce.

5. Bake for 10 minutes, or until just set. Sprinkle over the remaining pinch of pepper and serve hot.

Cook's tip: *Keep an eye on the Shakshouka as it cooks and take it out of the oven when the eggs are done to your liking – for very well done eggs it may need to be baked for up to 15 minutes.*

Capture the flavours and colours of Morocco with this spicy brown rice salad flecked with jewel-like dried apricots and glistening raisins and tossed with health-boosting kale.

Moroccan Chicken with Rice

PREP: 15 minutes
COOK: 35 minutes
SERVES: 4

250 g/9 oz easy-cook brown rice

2 tsp tomato purée

500 g/1 lb 2 oz skinless and boneless chicken breasts

85 g/3 oz ready-to-eat dried apricots, roughly chopped

55 g/2 oz raisins

55 g/2 oz preserved lemons, rinsed and finely chopped

1 small red onion, finely chopped

3 tbsp pine nuts

85 g/3 oz kale, shredded

Dressing

2 tsp rose harissa

4 tbsp olive oil

juice of 1 lemon

pinch of sea salt

pinch of pepper

1. Put the rice into a saucepan and cover with boiling water. Bring back to the boil, then simmer for 25—30 minutes, or until just tender. Drain, then transfer to a salad bowl.

2. Meanwhile, for the dressing, put the harissa, oil and lemon juice in a jam jar and season with the salt and pepper. Screw on the lid and shake well.

3. Spoon 2 tablespoons of the dressing into a bowl and mix in the tomato purée. Preheat the grill to high and line the grill pan with foil. Put the chicken on the foil in a single layer. Brush some of the tomato dressing over it, then grill for 15–18 minutes, or until golden and cooked through, turning and brushing with the remaining tomato dressing halfway through. Cut through the middle of a breast to check that the meat is no longer pink. Any juices that run out should be clear and piping hot with steam rising. Cover and leave to cool.

4. Drizzle the remaining dressing over the rice. Add the dried apricots, raisins, preserved lemons and red onion, then toss and leave to cool. Toast the pine nuts in a frying pan over a medium heat for 2–3 minutes. Blanch the kale for 2–3 minutes. Add the pine nuts and kale to the salad and stir. Thinly slice the chicken, arrange it over the salad and serve.

Cook's tip: *Try to find unsulphured (dark) dried apricots rather than the sulphured (bright orange) ones, as they are more natural and fruity tasting.*

Spiced Vegetable & Halloumi Skewers

PREP: 25 minutes
COOK: 30 minutes
SERVES: 8

250 g/9 oz chestnut mushrooms,
    halved or quartered depending on size

250 g/9 oz halloumi, cut into
    15-mm/5/8-inch cubes

1 large aubergine, cut into
    2-cm/3/4-inch chunks

450 g/1 lb cherry tomatoes

1 tbsp ras el hanout

1 tsp sea salt flakes, plus a large pinch

3 tbsp olive oil

These spiced skewers make a great vegetarian option for barbecues and are perfect for a crowd. Consider serving them with a pile of flatbreads (page 174), Greek-style natural yogurt, Tahina Sauce (page 165) and Rose Harissa (page 154) for people to create their own wraps. You will need 16 wooden skewers for this recipe.

1. Preheat the oven to 180°C/350°F/Gas Mark 4. Soak 16 wooden skewers in water for 20 minutes, then drain well.

2. Put the mushrooms, halloumi, aubergine and cherry tomatoes in a large bowl and toss well. Add the ras el hanout, 1 teaspoon of salt and oil and toss again.

3. Thread the vegetables and halloumi onto the skewers in any combination, then place them on two large baking trays. Roast for 30 minutes, or until the vegetables are tender. Sprinkle with a large pinch of salt and serve two skewers per person.

Cook's tip: *If you wish, assemble the skewers in advance, and let them marinate for a few hours in the fridge before cooking.*

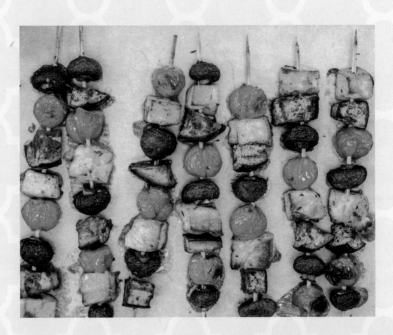

Warm Red Lentils with Spinach

PREP: 25 minutes
COOK: 30 minutes
SERVES: 4

2 tbsp olive oil

2 tsp cumin seeds

2 garlic cloves, crushed

2-cm/¾-inch piece of fresh
  ginger, peeled and finely grated

300 g/10½ oz red lentils

750 ml/1¼ pints hot vegetable stock

2 tbsp roughly chopped
  fresh mint

2 tbsp roughly chopped
  fresh coriander

2 red onions, thinly sliced

200 g/7 oz baby spinach

1 tsp hazelnut oil

150 g/5½ oz soft goat's cheese

4 tbsp Greek-style natural yogurt

pinch of pepper

This spiced, earthy salad is freshened up by the addition of mint and coriander leaves. It goes particularly well with Pomegranate Salad with Herbs & Pistachios (page 142).

1. Heat 1 tablespoon of the olive oil in a large saucepan over a medium heat. Add the cumin, garlic and ginger and stir-fry for 2 minutes. Stir in the lentils, then add the stock a ladleful at a time, simmering and stirring occasionally until each ladleful has been absorbed before adding the next one – this will take about 20 minutes in total. Remove from the heat, then stir in the mint and coriander.

2. Meanwhile, heat the remaining olive oil in a frying pan over a medium–low heat. Add the red onions and cook for 10 minutes, or until softened and lightly browned, stirring often.

3. Put the baby spinach and hazelnut oil in a bowl and toss gently. Divide between four shallow bowls.

4. Put the goat's cheese and yogurt in a small bowl, season with pepper, then mash.

5. Spoon the lentils onto the spinach, top with the onions, then spoon on the goat's cheese and yogurt and serve.

Cook's tip: *It's important not to overcook lentils for a salad, as they should have some bite.*

Okra is popular throughout the Middle East, and is served here in a Sephardi-inspired rich garlic, tomato and chickpea sauce. Roasting the okra separately helps prevent it from turning sticky.

Okra with Chickpeas, Tomatoes, Garlic & Onion

PREP: 25 minutes
COOK: 45 minutes
SERVES: 6

525 g/1 lb 3 oz okra

2 tsp sumac spice

grated zest and juice of
  1 unwaxed lemon

3 pinches of sea salt

2 pinches of pepper

4 tbsp olive oil

1 tsp coriander seeds

1 large onion, thinly sliced

500 g/1 lb 2 oz vine tomatoes,
  roughly chopped

2 garlic cloves, crushed

400 g/14 oz canned chickpeas in water,
  drained and rinsed

25 g/1 oz fresh coriander, roughly
  chopped, plus 1 tbsp to garnish

125 ml/4 fl oz water

1. Preheat the oven to 200°C/400°F/Gas Mark 6. Mix the okra, sumac, lemon zest, a pinch of salt and pepper and half the oil together in a roasting tin. Roast for 20 minutes, or until tender.

2. Meanwhile, heat the remaining oil in a frying pan over a low heat. Add the coriander seeds and fry for 2 minutes, or until aromatic. Increase the heat to medium–high, add the onion and a pinch of salt and fry for 10 minutes, or until golden brown, stirring occasionally.

3. Add the tomatoes and garlic to the onion and simmer for 5 minutes, breaking up any larger pieces of tomato using a wooden spoon. Add the chickpeas, fresh coriander and water, bring to the boil, then reduce the heat to a simmer, cover with a lid and cook for 15 minutes. Remove the lid and cook for a further 5 minutes, or until thickened.

4. Stir in the roast okra, then season with the lemon juice and a pinch of salt and pepper. Garnish with the remaining chopped fresh coriander and serve.

Cook's tip: *If you rinse okra before roasting it, be sure to dry it thoroughly with kitchen paper or it will steam rather than roast.*

These lightly spiced roast veg make a lovely light meal served with couscous or rice, and are just as good as a side dish for roast chicken or fish.

Cumin-roast Beetroot & Carrots with Tahini Dressing

PREP: 15 minutes
COOK: 1 hour
SERVES: 2

350 g/12 oz small raw beetroot, quartered

350 g/12 oz carrots, cut into wedges the same size as the beetroot quarters

1 tsp cumin seeds

1 tsp coriander seeds

1 tsp sea salt flakes

2 tbsp olive oil

20 g/¾ oz pistachio nuts, toasted and roughly chopped (see Cook's tip), to garnish

Dressing

1 tsp tahini

1 tbsp Greek-style natural yogurt

1 tbsp extra virgin olive oil

juice of ½ lemon

pinch of sea salt

1. Preheat the oven to 180°C/350°F/Gas Mark 4. Mix the beetroot, carrots, cumin, coriander, salt and olive oil together in a roasting tin. Roast for 1 hour, or until tender.

2. Meanwhile, for the dressing, whisk the tahini, yogurt, extra virgin olive oil and lemon juice together in a jug, then season with the salt.

3. Transfer the vegetables to a serving platter. Dot the dressing over them, scatter over the pistachio nuts and serve immediately.

Cook's tip: *To toast a large quantity of whole nuts, preheat your oven to 180°C/350°F/Gas Mark 4, spread the nuts onto a baking tray in a single layer, then roast for 5–10 minutes. Check them regularly as they burn easily. For smaller quantities of nuts, place them in a dry frying pan large enough to hold them in a single layer, and toast them over a low heat for 5–6 minutes, or until they are evenly golden and smell toasty, shaking the pan every couple of minutes. Do not leave them unattended – they will burn as soon as you turn your back.*

This dish is filling enough to eat as a vegetarian main course, but makes a great side dish for lamb or chicken too.

Spiced Roast Cauliflower with Almonds & Tahini Dressing

PREP: 10 minutes
COOK: 35 minutes
SERVES: 4

1 large cauliflower, cut into small florets

1 tsp baharat spice mix

1 tsp sea salt flakes

2 tbsp olive oil

25 g/1 oz blanched almonds, toasted, to garnish

3 tbsp roughly chopped fresh coriander, to garnish

Tahini dressing

20 g/¾ oz tahini

4 tbsp Greek-style natural yogurt

juice of ½ lemon

pinch of sea salt

pinch of pepper

1. Preheat the oven to 200°C/400°F/Gas Mark 6. Put the cauliflower in a large roasting tin. Sprinkle over the baharat spice mix, salt and oil and mix well. Roast for 25–35 minutes, or until lightly charred but still with some bite.

2. Meanwhile, for the dressing, mix the tahini, yogurt and lemon juice together in a bowl, then season with the salt and pepper.

3. Transfer the cauliflower to a serving plate, dot with the tahini dressing and scatter over the almonds and coriander. Serve immediately.

Cook's tip: *If you can't find baharat spice mix, use an equal mixture of ground coriander, ground cumin and ground cinnamon instead.*

Lebanese Seven-spice Roast Squash with Feta & Pine Nuts

PREP: 15 minutes
COOK: 45 minutes
SERVES: 6

1 x 1 kg/2 lb 4 oz butternut or other
   squash, halved and cut into wedges

2 tsp sea salt flakes, plus a pinch

2 tbsp extra virgin olive oil

pinch of pepper

30 g/1 oz pine nuts

75 g/2¾ oz feta cheese, crumbled

3 spring onions, thinly sliced

30 g/1 oz rocket

Lebanese seven-spice

1 tbsp pepper

1 tbsp ground allspice

1 tbsp ground cinnamon

1 tsp freshly grated nutmeg

1 tsp ground coriander

1 tsp ground cloves

1 tsp ground ginger

This is great for a crowd, and you can use whatever type of squash is in season. The crunchy spring onions and salty feta provide a lovely contrast to the smoky spiced squash.

1. Preheat the oven to 200°C/400°F/Gas Mark 6. For the Lebanese seven-spice, mix all the spices together in small bowl.

2. Put the squash in a roasting tin and scatter over 2 tablespoons of seven-spice and 2 teaspoons of salt, then drizzle with the oil and toss well using your hands. Roast for 45 minutes, or until tender. Leave to cool slightly, then season with a pinch of salt and pepper.

3. Toast the pine nuts in a frying pan over a medium heat for 2–3 minutes. Scatter them and the feta, spring onions and rocket over the squash, then serve immediately.

Cook's tip: *Rinse and dry the squash seeds, then scatter them into a frying pan with a teaspoon of seven-spice and dry-fry until golden. Sprinkle with sea salt. Use these instead of the pine nuts to top the dish, or eat as a snack. Keep any unused seven-spice in an airtight jar.*

There are numerous variations of batata harra, a spiced Lebanese potato dish. Although some include peppers and onions, this recipe is all about the moreish crispy potatoes, as they tend to lose their crunch once other vegetables are introduced. To finish the dish, herbs are fried in hot butter to bring out their flavour – a classic Middle Eastern technique.

Batata Harra

PREP: 10 minutes
COOK: 50 minutes
MARINATE: 1 hour
SERVES: 4

1 kg/2 lb 4 oz floury potatoes,
  such as Maris Piper,
  cut into 15-mm/⅝-inch chunks

3 garlic cloves, crushed

½ tsp cayenne pepper

2 tbsp olive oil

1 tsp sea salt flakes, plus a pinch

20 g/¾ oz butter

3 tbsp finely chopped fresh coriander

juice of ½ lemon

pinch of pepper

1. Mix the potatoes, garlic, cayenne and 1 tablespoon of the oil together in a large bowl. Cover and marinate in the refrigerator for at least 1 hour, or up to 4 hours.

2. When you are ready to cook, preheat the oven to 200°C/400°F/ Gas Mark 6. Tip the potatoes into a large roasting tin and if damp dry them with kitchen paper. Mix with another tablespoon of oil and a teaspoon of salt, then roast on a high shelf for 40–50 minutes, or until golden brown and crisp.

3. When the potatoes are cooked, heat the butter in a large frying pan over a low heat until it stops foaming. Stir in the coriander and fry for 1 minute. Tip in the roast potatoes, then add the lemon juice and toss. Season with a pinch of salt and pepper, then serve immediately.

Cook's tip: Herbs are often interchangeable in Middle Eastern recipes. In this dish coriander is a good match, but you can use fresh flat-leaf parsley if you prefer.

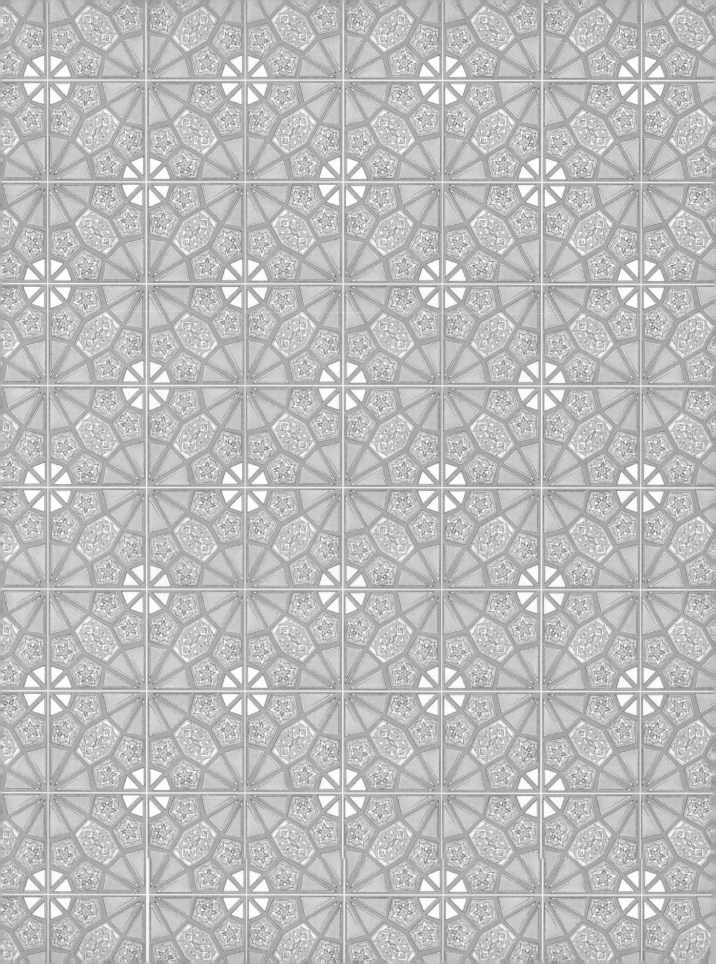

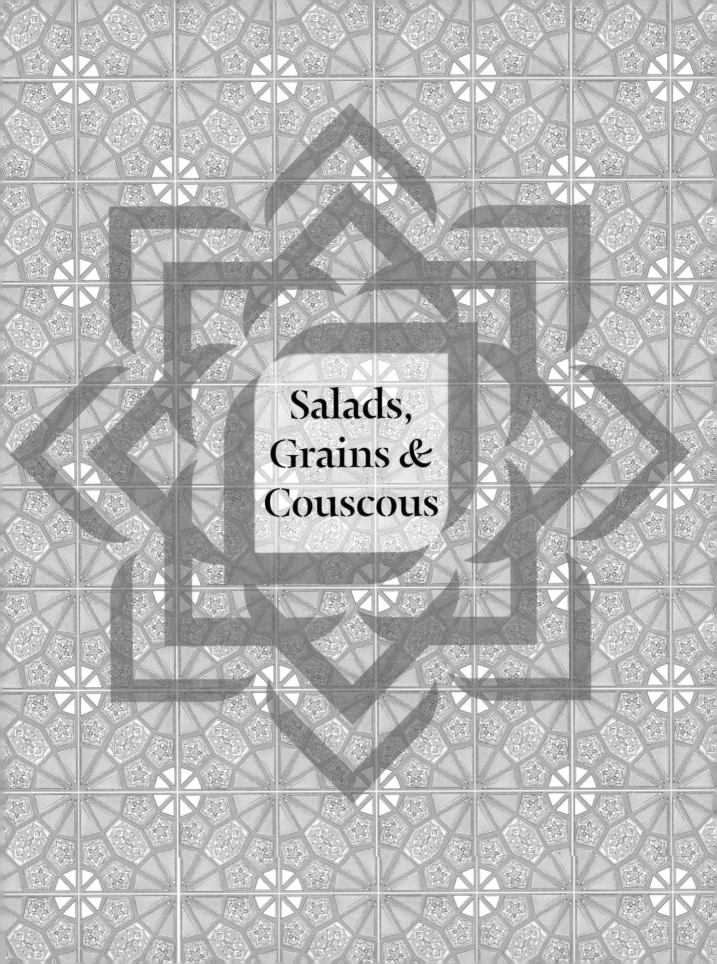

Salads,
Grains &
Couscous

Tabbouleh is a summery, fresh and aromatic green salad, in which soft herbs take centre stage and onion adds piquancy. It is served with many different dishes in the Middle East.

Classic Tabbouleh

PREP: 20 minutes
COOK: 10 minutes
SERVES: 6

40 g/1½ oz bulgur wheat, rinsed

100 g/3½ oz fresh flat-leaf parsley, very finely chopped

25 g/1 oz fresh mint, very finely chopped

½ onion, very finely chopped

250 g/9 oz vine tomatoes, very finely chopped

juice of ½ lemon

2 tbsp extra virgin olive oil

pinch of sea salt

pinch of pepper

1. Put the bulgur wheat in a saucepan and cover with four to five times its volume of boiling water. Bring to the boil, then reduce the heat and simmer uncovered for 8–10 minutes, or until cooked but with some bite. Drain, then rinse and tip into a large, shallow salad bowl. Leave to cool to room temperature.

2. Mix the parsley, mint, onion, tomatoes, lemon juice and oil into the bulgur wheat and season with the salt and pepper.

Cook's tip: *Customize your tabbouleh by adding very finely chopped fresh coriander, lovage or celery leaves.*

Chicken with Pomegranate & Beetroot Tabbouleh

PREP: 20 minutes
COOK: 30 minutes
SERVES: 4

225 g/8 oz wheatberries

350 g/12 oz raw beetroot,
  cut into cubes

500 g/1 lb 2 oz skinless, boneless
  chicken breasts, thinly sliced

1 small red onion, thinly sliced

200 g/7 oz cherry tomatoes, halved

1 small pomegranate, seeds only

2 tbsp roughly chopped fresh mint

70 g/2½ oz baby spinach

Dressing
juice of 1 lemon

4 tbsp extra virgin olive oil

2 garlic cloves, finely chopped

1 tsp light muscovado sugar

pinch of salt

pinch of pepper

This version of tabbouleh combines wholegrain wheatberries with traditional pomegranate for a modern twist on the classic Middle Eastern dish.

1. Half-fill the base of a steamer with water, bring to the boil, then add the wheatberries to the water. Put the beetroot in the steamer top, cover with a lid and steam for 20–25 minutes, or until the wheatberries and beetroot are tender. Drain the wheatberries.

2. Meanwhile, for the dressing, put the lemon juice, oil, garlic and sugar in a jam jar and season with the salt and pepper. Screw on the lid and shake well.

3. Put the chicken in a bowl, add half the dressing and toss well. Heat a griddle pan over a medium–high heat until smoking hot. Add the chicken and cook for 8–10 minutes, or until golden and cooked through, turning once or twice.

4. Put the red onion, cherry tomatoes and pomegranate seeds in a large shallow bowl. Add the wheatberries, beetroot and mint and toss. Divide the spinach between four plates, spoon the wheatberry mixture over them, then arrange the chicken on top. Serve with the remaining dressing in a small jug.

Chicken & Couscous Salad

PREP: 25 minutes
COOK: 20 minutes
SERVES: 4

175 g/6 oz giant wholewheat
   couscous

175 g/6 oz cooked beetroot in
   natural juices, drained and
   cut into cubes

1 small red onion, finely chopped

125 g/4½ oz cherry tomatoes, halved

1 pomegranate, seeds only

juice of 2 lemons

2 tbsp flaxseed (linseed) oil

2 tbsp olive oil

4 tsp tomato purée

pinch of sea salt

pinch of pepper

2 tbsp roughly chopped fresh mint

1 tsp black peppercorns, crushed

500 g/1 lb 2 oz chicken breast mini
   fillets, thinly sliced

The beetroot in this salad turns everything a deep, vibrant red and glistens jewel-like with the pomegranate seeds.

1. Put the giant couscous in a saucepan and cover with boiling water. Bring back to the boil, then simmer for 6–8 minutes, or until just tender. Drain, then rinse and tip into a shallow salad bowl. Add the beetroot, then the red onion, cherry tomatoes and pomegranate seeds.

2. For the dressing, put the juice of one lemon, the flaxseed oil, half the olive oil and half the tomato purée in a jam jar and season with the salt and pepper, screw on the lid and shake well. Drizzle over the salad, then sprinkle over the mint and toss.

3. Put the remaining lemon juice, olive oil and tomato purée and the crushed peppercorns in a clean plastic bag, twist and shake well. Add the chicken, seal, then shake until it is evenly coated.

4. Heat a griddle pan over a medium–high heat until smoking hot. Add the chicken and cook for 8–10 minutes, or until golden and cooked through, turning once or twice. Arrange over the salad and serve.

Bulgur wheat is a popular alternative to rice in many parts of the Middle East, particularly Syria and the Lebanon. This is a lovely, filling vegetarian main course and perfect for a lunchbox.

Bulgur Wheat Salad with Roast Carrots, Mint & Almonds

PREP: 15 minutes
COOK: 40 minutes
SERVES: 4

800 g/1 lb 12 oz carrots, cut into small wedges

2 tsp cumin seeds

2 tsp ground ginger

2 tsp sea salt flakes

4 tbsp olive oil

250 g/9 oz bulgur wheat, rinsed and drained

100 g/3½ oz blanched almonds, toasted

40 g/1½ oz fresh mint, roughly chopped

juice of 1 lemon

large pinch of pepper

1. Preheat the oven to 200°C/400°F/Gas Mark 6. Mix the carrots, cumin, ginger, salt and 3 tablespoons of the oil together in a roasting tin. Roast for 40 minutes, or until tender.

2. Meanwhile, put the bulgur wheat in a saucepan and cover with three to four times its volume of boiling water. Bring to the boil, then reduce the heat and simmer uncovered for 8–10 minutes, or until cooked but with some bite. Drain into a sieve, then pour in the remaining 1 tablespoon of oil and mix. Leave it to steam dry in the sieve for a few minutes.

3. Tip the bulgur wheat into the roasting tin with the cooked carrots. Add the almonds, mint, lemon juice and pepper and mix well. Transfer to a bowl and serve hot or cold.

Cook's tip: To add extra veg to this dish, roast any of your favourite root veg with the carrots, or mix in chopped fresh baby spinach with the mint in step three. You could also add crumbled feta just before serving.

Light and summery, this couscous can be served with almost any Middle Eastern dish. It is the perfect accompaniment to grilled fish or fish tagines, as the herbs and lemon complement fish beautifully.

Summer Couscous with Herbs & Preserved Lemons

PREP: 15 minutes
COOK: 25 minutes
SERVES: 4

350 g/12 oz couscous

400 ml/14 fl oz boiling water

½ tsp sea salt flakes

2 tbsp olive oil

4 spring onions, finely chopped or thinly sliced

6 tbsp finely chopped fresh flat-leaf parsley

6 tbsp finely chopped fresh mint

6 tbsp finely chopped fresh coriander

15 g/½ oz butter

½ preserved lemon, rinsed and finely chopped

1. Preheat the oven to 180°C/350°F/Gas Mark 4. Tip the couscous into an ovenproof bowl. Pour the boiling water into a jug, stir in the salt, then pour it over the couscous, place a folded tea towel over the top and set aside for 10 minutes, or until the couscous is tender and the liquid has been absorbed.

2. Drizzle the oil over the couscous. Using your fingers, rub it into the grains to break up the lumps. Toss in the spring onions and half the herbs. Dot the surface with the butter and cover with foil or wet greaseproof paper. Bake for 15 minutes.

3. Fluff up the couscous using a fork, then tip it into a large salad bowl. Toss the remaining herbs into the couscous and scatter the preserved lemon over the top. Serve hot.

Cook's tip: *Fluffing up couscous is very important as it not only removes lumps, but also aerates the grains.*

Grilling aubergines until blackened all over gives this dressing a wonderfully smoky flavour. Alternatively, they can be barbecued or roasted in a hot oven.

Red Cabbage & Baby Leaf Salad

PREP: 30 minutes
COOK: 20 minutes
SERVES: 4

2 carrots, shredded into ribbons using a swivel-bladed vegetable peeler

350 g/12 oz red cabbage, shredded

55 g/2 oz raisins

125 g/4½ oz bistro salad (a mix of red-stemmed baby red chard, bull's blood chard and lamb's lettuce)

juice of 1 orange

pinch of pepper

Dressing

3 aubergines

3 garlic cloves, finely chopped

2 tbsp tahini

3 tbsp hemp oil

pinch of pepper

1. For the dressing, preheat the grill to high and remove the grill rack. Prick both ends of each aubergine using a fork, put them in the grill pan and grill 5 cm/2 inches away from the heat source for 15–20 minutes, or until blackened, turning several times. Leave to cool.

2. Arrange the carrots on a serving plate, top with the cabbage, then sprinkle over the raisins and bistro salad. Drizzle with the orange juice and season with the pepper.

3. Cut the aubergines in half lengthways and scoop the soft flesh away from the blackened skins and onto a chopping board using a dessert spoon. Discard the skin. Finely chop the flesh, then put it in a bowl. Add the garlic, tahini and hemp oil, season with the pepper and mix. Spoon into a serving bowl and nestle in the centre of the salad to serve.

Cook's tip: *When grilling aubergines it is essential to cook them until they are black all over and the flesh is soft.*

Fennel is delicious with orange. This salad works well with Whole Spice-crusted Red Snapper (page 70).

Quinoa Salad with Fennel & Orange

PREP: 20 minutes
COOK: 12 minutes
SERVES: 4

900 ml/1½ pints hot vegetable stock

225 g/8 oz quinoa, rinsed

3 oranges

250 g/9 oz fennel, thinly sliced using a mandolin, green feathery tops reserved and torn into small pieces

2 spring onions, finely chopped

3 tbsp roughly chopped fresh flat-leaf parsley

Dressing
juice of ½ lemon

3 tbsp extra virgin olive oil

pinch of pepper

1. Pour the stock into a saucepan and bring to the boil. Add the quinoa, then reduce the heat and simmer uncovered for 10–12 minutes, or until the germs separate from the seeds. Drain into a sieve, then tip the quinoa into a salad bowl and leave to cool to room temperature.

2. Grate the zest from two of the oranges and put it in a jam jar. Cut any remaining peel and the pith away from all three oranges using a small serrated knife and discard. Hold each orange above a bowl and cut between the membranes to release the segments. Squeeze the juice from the membranes into the jam jar.

3. Add the orange segments, fennel slices, spring onions and parsley to the quinoa.

4. For the dressing, add the lemon juice and oil to the jam jar and season with the pepper. Screw on the lid and shake well.

5. Drizzle the dressing over the salad and toss. Garnish with the fennel fronds and serve immediately.

Cook's tip: *It is much easier to thinly slice using a mandolin, but a small, very sharp knife will also do the job.*

This light, fresh salad is perfect for late spring or summer lunches. Dill is popular throughout the Middle East, particularly in Iran and Turkey, where it is often paired with broad beans in a variety of dishes. If serving this salad on its own, it's lovely scattered with crumbled feta, or it's a wonderful accompaniment to Roast Salmon with Spices, Pomegranate & Coriander (page 84).

Freekeh, Broad Bean & Pea Salad with Dill & Pomegranate

PREP: 15 minutes
COOK: 50 minutes
SERVES: 4

175 g/6 oz wholegrain freekeh

600 ml/1 pint water

100 g/3½ oz peas

100 g/3½ oz podded broad beans

3 spring onions, thinly sliced

3 tbsp finely chopped fresh dill

3 tbsp finely chopped fresh mint

grated zest and juice of 1 unwaxed
   lemon, plus extra squeeze of juice

2 tbsp extra virgin olive oil

pinch of sea salt

pinch of pepper

85 g/3 oz feta cheese, crumbled (optional)

½ pomegranate, seeds only

1. Rinse the freekeh in several changes of cold water. Tip it into a saucepan, cover with the water and bring to the boil. Reduce the heat and simmer, covered, for 45–50 minutes, or until cooked but with some bite. Drain well.

2. Blanch the peas and broad beans in boiling water for 1 minute, then drain, refresh in cold water and drain again. Add them to the freekeh.

3. Mix the spring onions, dill, mint and lemon zest into the salad. Stir in the oil and lemon juice and season with the salt and pepper, adding extra lemon juice if you wish.

4. Serve the salad warm, scattered with the feta, if using, and pomegranate seeds.

Cook's tip: Freekeh is young, green wheat that has been harvested early and then toasted and cracked. It has been cooked in the Middle East since ancient times.

Sweet tomatoes, crisp salty pitta chips, crunchy radish and cucumber, and a citrus dressing come together in this traditional Levantine salad. Use the best vine or heritage tomatoes that you can find.

Fattoush

PREP: 15 minutes
COOK: 12 minutes
SERVES: 6–8

700 g/1 lb 9 oz mixed vine and heritage tomatoes, roughly chopped

100 g/3½ oz radishes, thinly sliced

200 g/7 oz cucumber, roughly chopped

3 spring onions, thinly sliced

3 large pinches of sea salt

pinch of pepper

2 tbsp olive oil

200 g/7 oz wholemeal pitta bread, cut or torn into triangles

125 g/4½ oz mixed salad leaves

Dressing

2 tbsp extra virgin olive oil

juice of ½ lemon

1 tsp sumac spice

1. Mix the tomatoes, radishes, cucumber, spring onions and a pinch of salt and pepper together in a large shallow salad bowl using your hands.

2. Line a plate with kitchen paper. Heat the oil in a large, heavy frying pan over a medium heat. Working in batches, fry the pitta bread for 4–6 minutes, or until crisp and golden, turning halfway through. Transfer to the prepared plate and sprinkle with the remaining salt. Repeat until you have fried all the pittas.

3. For the dressing, put all the ingredients in a jam jar, screw on the lid and shake well.

4. Add the salad leaves and pitta chips to the salad bowl. Drizzle the dressing over the salad and toss. Serve immediately.

Cook's tip: *If you're preparing this salad in advance, keep the dressing, leaves, tomato mixture and pitta chips separate, and combine just before serving.*

This light salad makes an elegant starter, light lunch or dinner. It also works well as a side dish for Lamb Kofte with Yogurt & Mint Dip (page 66), Whole Spice-crusted Red Snapper (page 70) or Ras el Hanout, Garlic & Thyme Roast Leg of Lamb (page 82).

Fig, Goat's Cheese & Watercress Salad

PREP: 10 minutes
SERVES: 4

6 figs, halved lengthways

85 g/3 oz watercress

60 g/2¼ oz soft goat's cheese

40 g/1½ oz blanched almonds, toasted

Dressing

2 tbsp finely chopped fresh mint

juice of ½ lemon

1 tbsp runny honey

1 tbsp extra virgin olive oil

pinch of sea salt

pinch of pepper

1. For the dressing, whisk the mint, lemon juice, honey and oil together in a small jug and season with the salt and pepper.

2. Put the figs in a small bowl, drizzle over a tablespoon of the dressing and mix gently.

3. Pile the watercress onto a large serving plate. Drizzle the dressing over the salad and toss. Scatter the figs, goat's cheese and almonds over the watercress. Serve immediately.

Cook's tip: *You can substitute other young salad leaves, such as spinach, rocket or baby chard, for the watercress in this salad, or use a mixture if you prefer.*

Pickled vegetables are popular in the Middle East, and it takes just 30 minutes to lightly pickle your own beetroot. The soft goat's cheese contrasts beautifully with the crisp beetroot and sharp grapefruit.

Pickled Beetroot, Grapefruit & Goat's Cheese Salad

PREP: 20 minutes
MARINATE: 30 minutes
SERVES: 4

600 g/1 lb 5 oz raw beetroot, peeled and very thinly sliced using a mandolin

3 tbsp white wine or cider vinegar

2 pinches of sea salt flakes

2 pink grapefruit, peeled and segmented

125 g/4½ oz soft goat's cheese, cut into cubes

50 g/1¾ oz blanched almonds, toasted

4 tbsp roughly chopped fresh dill

Dressing

2 tbsp extra virgin olive oil

2 tbsp runny honey

2 tbsp grapefruit juice

pinch of pepper

1 Mix the beetroot, vinegar and a pinch of salt together in a large bowl. Cover and leave to marinate for 30 minutes.

2. For the dressing, whisk the oil, honey and grapefruit juice together in a small jug and season with a pinch of salt and pepper.

3. Pile the pickled beetroot, grapefruit, goat's cheese, almonds and dill onto a platter. Drizzle the dressing over the salad and toss. Serve immediately.

Cook's tip: *For an even more colourful dish, look out for golden or candy beetroot when it's in season.*

This refreshing, crunchy summer salad has a lovely balance of sweetness from the watermelon and saltiness from the feta, brought together beautifully by the lively mint dressing. Serve it as part of an outdoor summer salad spread on a hot day, box it up for picnics, or enjoy it on a gloomy day to give instant indoor sunshine.

Summer Watermelon, Feta & Mint Salad

PREP: 15 minutes
SERVES: 4

300 g/10½ oz watermelon flesh,
   cut into 2-cm/¾-inch cubes
300 g/10½ oz cucumber,
   cut into 2-cm/¾-inch cubes
175 g/6 oz feta cheese,
   cut into 2-cm/¾-inch cubes
5 g/⅛ oz fresh mint leaves

Dressing
4 tbsp shredded fresh mint
juice of 1 lemon
2 tbsp olive oil
pinch of sea salt
pinch of pepper

1. Mix the watermelon, cucumber and feta together in a large bowl. Add the whole mint leaves.

2. For the dressing, whisk the shredded mint, lemon juice and oil together in a small jug and season with the salt and pepper.

3. Drizzle the dressing over the salad and toss, being careful the feta doesn't break up. Serve immediately.

Cook's tip: *If preparing this salad in advance, keep the watermelon, cucumber and feta refrigerated in three separate containers. Make the dressing and store it in a fourth container. Combine all four elements just before serving to avoid the salad becoming watery.*

This refreshing, crunchy salad puts pomegranate centre stage rather than using it as a garnish. It makes a delicious and unusual part of a meze meal, but also works as an accompaniment to Chicken, Mushroom & Lemon Borekas (page 184) or Beef Sambousek (page 186).

Pomegranate Salad with Herbs & Pistachios

PREP: 10 minutes
SERVES: 4

2 large pomegranates, seeds only

6 tbsp finely chopped fresh coriander

6 tbsp finely chopped fresh flat-leaf parsley

4 tbsp finely chopped fresh mint

30 g/1 oz unsalted pistachio nuts, halved

2 tbsp extra virgin olive oil

juice of ½ lemon

1. Put the pomegranate seeds, coriander, parsley, mint and pistachio nuts in a large salad bowl and mix well.

2. Pour over the oil and squeeze over the lemon juice, then stir and serve.

Cook's tip: *You can prepare this salad in advance, then cover it and chill in the refrigerator. It is best eaten within a few hours of being made.*

This fresh, summery dish is lovely as part of a meze meal or served as an accompaniment to roast chicken. 'Smashing' the cucumber instead of slicing it gives the salad an unusual texture.

Cucumber, Radish & Sesame Salad with Lemon & Dill Dressing

PREP: 10 minutes
CHILL: 1 hour
SERVES: 4

1 cucumber, cut into 5-cm/2-inch rounds
large pinch of sea salt
6 radishes, thinly sliced
5 tsp sesame seeds

Dressing
juice of 1 lemon
2 tbsp pink peppercorns, crushed
4 tbsp extra virgin olive oil
1 tsp tahini
2 tbsp finely chopped fresh dill
large pinch of sea salt

1. Put the cucumber in a large freezer bag and seal. Using a rolling pin, gently smash it into large, irregular chunks, then tip them into a colander. Add a large pinch of salt and shake. Set over a bowl and transfer to the refrigerator for 1 hour, or until drained and firmed up.

2. Meanwhile, for the dressing, whisk all the ingredients together in a small jug.

3. Mix the cucumber, radishes and sesame seeds together in a salad bowl. Drizzle the dressing over the salad and toss. Serve immediately.

Cook's tip: *Cucumber salads often taste watery, but by salting the cucumber for an hour you make sure it stays crisp and crunchy.*

Couscous combined with dried fruit and nuts is delicious served with grilled meats and spicy tagines. Traditionally, a fruity couscous would also be dusted with cinnamon and served on its own, often as a palate cleanser.

Spicy Couscous with Nuts, Dates & Apricots

PREP: 15 minutes
COOK: 10 minutes
SERVES: 4

350 g/12 oz couscous

400 ml/14 fl oz boiling water

½ tsp sea salt flakes

2 tbsp olive oil

12 tbsp clarified butter

large pinch of saffron threads

115 g/4 oz blanched almonds

115 g/4 oz unsalted pistachio nuts

1–2 tsp ras el hanout

115 g/4 oz dates, thinly sliced

115 g/4 oz ready-to-eat dried apricots, thinly sliced

2 tsp ground cinnamon, to garnish

1. Tip the couscous into a shallow heatproof bowl. Put the boiling water in a jug, stir in the salt, then pour it over the couscous, cover and leave for 10 minutes.

2. Drizzle the oil over the couscous. Using your fingers, rub it into the grains to break up the lumps.

3. Heat the butter in a heavy-based frying pan over a medium heat. Add the saffron, almonds and pistachio nuts and cook for 1–2 minutes, or until the nuts begin to brown and emit a nutty aroma, stirring occasionally. Stir in the ras el hanout, toss in the dates and dried apricots and cook, stirring, for 2 minutes. Fluff up the couscous using a fork, then tip it into the pan, mix well and heat through. Remove from the heat.

4. Pile the couscous onto a serving plate in a mound. Rub the cinnamon through your fingers to create vertical lines from the top of the mound to the base, like the spokes of a wheel. Serve immediately.

Cook's tip: *Choose moist dates to ensure the salad is not dry.*

Dips,
Preserves
& Sauces

This popular Levantine aubergine dip is incredibly easy to make, and a perfect complement to freshly made pitta breads (page 172). This is the Egyptian version, made with tahini and lemon juice. Other versions include slowly fried onions and tomatoes.

Baba Ghanouj

PREP: 15 minutes
COOK: 1 hour
SERVES: 4

1 large aubergine

juice of 1 lemon

½ garlic clove, crushed

2 tsp tahini

large pinch of sea salt

2 tbsp extra virgin olive oil

1 tbsp roughly chopped fresh flat-leaf parsley (optional)

pitta breads, to serve (optional)

½ cucumber, cut into large batons, to serve (optional)

1. Preheat the grill to medium–high and remove the grill rack. Prick the aubergine all over using a fork, put it in the grill pan and grill 5 cm/2 inches away from the heat source for 30 minutes on each side, or until soft and blackened all over and almost falling apart. Leave to cool.

2. Cut the aubergine in half lengthways and scoop the soft flesh away from the blackened skin and into a bowl using a dessert spoon. Discard the skin. Mash the flesh using a fork, then stir in the lemon juice, garlic, tahini, salt and 1 tablespoon of oil.

3. Spoon the dip into a serving bowl, then drizzle with the remaining oil and sprinkle over the parsley, if using. Serve with pitta breads and cucumber batons, if using.

Cook's tip: It's always a good idea to taste food just before serving and adjust the balance of flavourings if you wish. You may like to add a little more lemon juice, sea salt or garlic to this dip.

Rose
Harissa
page 154

Homemade harissa is fresher and more vibrant than shop-bought, and you can control the amount of chilli, oil and seasoning you include.

Rose Harissa

PREP: 15 minutes
COOK 3 minutes
SERVES: 10

2 tsp cumin seeds

1 tsp coriander seeds

1 tsp fennel seeds

8 red chillies, roughly chopped

½ large red pepper, deseeded and roughly chopped

6 garlic cloves

¼ tsp rosewater

2 tbsp olive oil

2 tsp sea salt flakes, plus a pinch

2 tbsp dried rose petals

1. Heat a small frying pan over a low heat. Add the cumin, coriander and fennel seeds and toast for 2–3 minutes, or until aromatic. Tip into a pestle and mortar and crush to a powder.

2. Put the chillies, including the seeds, the red pepper, garlic, rosewater, oil, 2 teaspoons of salt, the spice powder and half the rose petals in a blender and whizz until they form a paste with the consistency of homemade pesto – it should not be completely smooth. Stir in the remaining rose petals and season with a pinch of salt.

3. The harissa can be kept, covered, in the refrigerator for 3–4 days.

› **Pictured on previous page**

Cook's tip: If you prefer a thicker harissa paste, reduce the amount of oil by half. If you prefer a more sauce-like consistency, drizzle in more oil and adjust the seasoning accordingly. You can increase or decrease the number of chillies to taste.

This fresh, spiced yogurt dip is lovely served in little lettuce leaves for a starter, or as a dip to go with crudités.

Spiced Beetroot & Cucumber Cacik

PREP: 20 minutes
SERVES: 4

115 g/4 oz cooked beetroot in natural juices (drained weight), drained and cut into cubes

150 g/5½ oz cucumber, cut into small cubes

40 g/1½ oz radishes, cut into small cubes

1 spring onion, finely chopped

12 Little Gem lettuce leaves

Dip

150 g/5½ oz low-fat Greek-style natural yogurt

¼ tsp ground cumin

½ tsp runny honey

2 tbsp finely chopped fresh mint

pinch of salt

pinch of pepper

1. For the dip, put the yogurt, cumin and honey in a large bowl. Stir in the mint and season with the salt and pepper.

2. Add the beetroot, cucumber, radishes and spring onion, then toss.

3. Arrange the lettuce leaves on a plate. Spoon a little of the salad into each leaf. Serve immediately.

› **Pictured overleaf**

Cook's tip: When spooning honey, heat the metal spoon so that the honey comes off more easily.

Spiced
Beetroot &
Cucumber
Cacik
page 155

This Syrian red pepper and walnut dip is popular throughout the Levant. It's somewhere between a thick hummus and an Italian pesto in texture. It's delicious scooped up with hot, crisp pitta breads (page 172).

Muhammara

PREP: 25 minutes
COOK: 1 hour 10 minutes
SERVES: 6

3 red peppers

60 g/2¼ oz walnuts

30 g/1 oz fresh or dried breadcrumbs

1 tbsp pomegranate molasses

1 tsp sea salt flakes

4 tbsp extra virgin olive oil

juice of ½ lemon

pinch of dried red chilli flakes

1. Preheat the grill to medium–high and remove the grill rack. Line the grill pan with foil. Put the red peppers in the lined pan and grill 5 cm/2 inches away from the heat source for 1 hour, or until blackened, turning occasionally.

2. Preheat the oven to 180°C/350°F/Gas Mark 4. Transfer the hot peppers to a bowl, cover with clingfilm and set aside for 10 minutes to help steam off the skins.

3. Meanwhile, scatter the walnuts and breadcrumbs on a baking tray in a single layer and roast for 10 minutes, or until golden brown. Check them regularly as they burn easily. Leave them to cool to room temperature.

4. Peel the skins off the peppers and remove and discard the stalks and seeds while retaining the juices. Put the peppers, walnuts, breadcrumbs, pomegranate molasses, salt, oil, lemon juice and chilli flakes in a food processor and whizz until smooth. Spoon into a bowl and serve as a dip.

Cook's tip: *We all have an individual preference for balance of saltiness, sweetness, acidity and bitterness. Taste the Muhammara once blended, and adjust the consistency and taste with more olive oil, lemon juice or salt as required.*

Hummus with Garlic Toasts

PREP: 10 minutes
COOK: 3 minutes
SERVES: 4

400 g/14 oz canned chickpeas
  in water, drained with a little
  of the liquid reserved
juice of 1 large lemon
6 tbsp tahini
2 tbsp olive oil
2 garlic cloves, crushed
pinch of sea salt
pinch of pepper
1 tbsp finely chopped
  fresh coriander
2 tbsp Kalamata olives,
  stoned, to garnish

Ciabatta toasts
1 ciabatta loaf, sliced
2 garlic cloves, crushed
1 tbsp chopped fresh coriander
4 tbsp olive oil

This makes a perfect quick and easy lunch served with pitta breads (page 172) and is delicious as an accompaniment to a spread of Middle Eastern salads.

1. For the hummus, put the chickpeas and a little of their reserved liquid in a food processor and whizz, gradually adding more of the reserved liquid and the lemon juice until you have the consistency you desire. Blend well after each addition, until smooth.

2. Stir in the tahini and all but 1 teaspoon of the oil. Add the garlic, season with the salt and pepper, and whizz again until smooth.

3. Spoon the hummus into a serving dish. Drizzle the remaining oil over the top and garnish with the coriander and olives. Cover and chill in the refrigerator while preparing the ciabatta toasts.

4. Preheat the grill to medium–high. Lay the ciabatta on the grill rack in a single layer. Mix the garlic, coriander and oil together and drizzle over the bread. Cook for 2–3 minutes, or until golden brown, turning once. Serve hot with the hummus.

Broad Bean & Mint Hummus

PREP: 20 minutes
COOK: 10 minutes
SERVES: 4

350 g/12 oz broad beans (podded weight)

2 tbsp extra virgin olive oil

1 tsp cumin seeds, crushed

3 spring onions, thinly sliced

2 garlic cloves, finely chopped

25 g/1 oz fresh mint, torn into pieces

5 tbsp finely chopped fresh flat-leaf
   parsley

juice of 1 lemon

4 tbsp Greek-style natural yogurt

pinch of sea salt

pinch of pepper

To serve

1 red pepper and 1 yellow pepper,
   deseeded and cut into strips

4 celery sticks, cut into strips

½ cucumber, halved, deseeded
   and cut into strips

4 wholemeal pitta breads

This summery hummus, made with freshly podded broad beans flavoured with chopped fresh herbs and lemon juice, is delicious on warm pitta bread (page 172).

1. Half-fill the base of a steamer with water, bring to the boil, then put the beans in the steamer top, cover with a lid and steam for 10 minutes, or until tender.

2. Meanwhile, heat the oil in a frying pan over a medium heat. Add the cumin, spring onions and garlic and fry for 2 minutes, or until the onions are softened.

3. Put the beans in a food processor, add the onion mixture, mint, parsley, lemon juice, yogurt, salt and pepper. Whizz to a coarse purée, then spoon into a dish set on a large plate.

4. Arrange the vegetable strips around the hummus and serve with the pittas.

Cook's tip: *You will need to buy about 750 g/1 lb 10 oz broad beans in their pods to get about 350 g/12 oz when podded.*

This piquant green Yemeni chilli sauce goes well with boiled eggs, as a dip for Chicken, Mushroom & Lemon Borekas (page 184) or Beef Sambousek (page 186), or as a sauce to cut through the richness of roast lamb. It takes minutes to prepare in a food processor.

Zhoug

PREP: 15 minutes
SERVES: 6

40 g/1½ oz fresh coriander,
 roughly chopped

2 tbsp roughly chopped
 fresh flat-leaf parsley

1 preserved lemon, rinsed
 and roughly chopped

1 garlic clove

6 green cardamom pods, seeds only

2 green chillies, deseeded if you
 prefer a less spicy sauce,
 and roughly chopped

½ tsp caster sugar

½ tsp ground cumin

5 tbsp extra virgin olive oil

1 tsp sea salt flakes

1. Put all the ingredients in a food processor or blender and whizz until you have a smooth sauce. Season with extra salt if you wish.

2. The sauce can be kept covered in the refrigerator for up to 3 days.

Cook's tip: If you do not have a food processor, very finely chop the coriander, parsley and preserved lemon and tip them into a bowl. Crush the garlic, cardamom seeds and green chillies together in a pestle and mortar and add them to the herbs. Stir in the sugar, cumin, extra virgin olive oil, salt and 2 tablespoons of water and mix well.

Labneh

PREP: 5 minutes
DRAIN: 4 hours
SERVES: 4

500 g/1 lb 2 oz Greek-style
  natural yogurt
½ tsp sea salt flakes

Labneh is easy to make, and delicious drizzled with good-quality olive oil and sprinkled with sea salt and herbs as part of a meze meal. It's equally good served with desserts such as Roast Figs with Honey and Thyme (page 197) as an alternative to clotted cream. You will need a clean, damp muslin, a rubber band and some string for this recipe.

1. Line a sieve with damp muslin or clean kitchen cloth, then place it over a bowl. Mix the yogurt with the salt and put it in the prepared sieve. Bring the edges of the cloth up and gently twist them together to enclose the yogurt into a ball. You don't need to twist very tightly, just enough to hold the yogurt mix firmly. Secure the twist with a rubber band.

2. Leave the yogurt to drain for 4 hours; it should have the consistency of very thick cream cheese. The labneh can be kept in the refrigerator, covered, for up to 2 days.

Cook's tip: *If you like labneh to have a firmer texture, let it hang overnight in the fridge. For quicker results, hang it on a cupboard door handle using a piece of string, with a bowl set underneath it to catch the liquid.*

Tahina Sauce

PREP: 10 minutes
SERVES: 6

1 tsp cumin seeds

3 garlic cloves

75 g/2¾ oz tahini

5 tbsp iced water

juice of 1 lemon

2 tsp sea salt flakes, plus a pinch

pinch of pepper

As anyone who has tried to scrape the last spoonful from the jar knows, tahini (or ground sesame) paste is far too thick to use as a sauce. This popular Middle Eastern condiment blends it with lemon juice, garlic and water to form a light sauce, which is perfect for slathering over wraps or into stuffed pitta breads. Try it with Spicy Grilled Chicken Wraps (page 58) or as an accompaniment to Kibbeh (page 18).

1. Heat a small frying pan over a low heat. Add the cumin seeds and toast for 2–3 minutes, or until aromatic. Tip into a pestle and mortar and crush to a powder.

2. Put the ground cumin, garlic, tahini, iced water, lemon juice and 2 teaspoons of salt in a blender and whizz until smooth. You want the consistency of single cream. Season with a pinch of salt and pepper and add more lemon juice if you wish.

3. The sauce can be kept in the refrigerator, covered, for 2–3 days.

Cook's tip: *The amount of garlic in the recipe gives the sauce a strong kick. If you prefer a milder garlic flavour, start with one clove, blitz, and add more if you wish.*

It's well worth having a stash of home-made preserved lemons in the fridge – they're really easy to make. Use them to jazz up all sorts of dishes, from baked fish to roast vegetables.

Preserved Lemons

PREP: 20 minutes
PRESERVE: 3 weeks
MAKES: 8 lemons

8 unwaxed lemons, washed and dried

8 tbsp sea salt flakes

1 tbsp coriander seeds

1 bay leaf

1. Preheat the oven to 140°C/275°F/Gas Mark 1. Wash a 1-litre/1¾-pint jar in hot, soapy water, then rinse well. Place the jar on a baking tray and put it in the oven to dry completely. If using a kilner jar, remove and boil the rubber seal.

2. Using the palm of your hand, roll each lemon hard on the work surface to release its juices.

3. Using a very sharp knife, cut a small disc from the stem end of each lemon, then stand the lemons upright. Cut a deep X-shape through each lemon, stopping 1 cm/½ inch from the base, then stuff each one with 1 tablespoon of salt.

4. Pack the lemons tightly into the jar, adding the coriander seeds and bay leaf as you go, and push them down well. If the lemons are small, add a few more following the method above to make sure they're squashed in before sealing the jar.

5. Set aside at room temperature. After 3 days, the jar should be full of liquid – if not, top up with fresh lemon juice. Leave to steep at room temperature for 3 weeks. The preserved lemons can be kept in the refrigerator for up to 6 months.

Cook's tip: *Once your preserved lemons are ready to eat, rinse them well in cold water before using them. You can thinly slice the peel and add it to dishes, or mash the pulp through a sieve and use the juice as a seasoning.*

Throughout the Middle East, pickled vegetables are served with meze dishes. Turnips are traditional, but other pale vegetables, such as cabbage and cauliflower, can be given the same colourful treatment.

Pickled Turnips

PREP: 25 minutes
COOK: 5 minutes
PRESERVE: 2 weeks
MAKES: about 500 g/1 lb 2 oz

500 g/1 lb 2 oz turnips, trimmed

1 small cooked beetroot in natural juices, drained and thinly sliced

1 fresh bay leaf

Pickling brine

300 ml/10 fl oz water

150 ml/5 fl oz white wine vinegar or cider vinegar

2 tbsp sea salt flakes

4 garlic cloves, thinly sliced

1 tsp coriander seeds, crushed

½ tsp dried red chilli flakes (optional)

1. Preheat the oven to 140°C/275°F/Gas Mark 1. Wash a 750-ml/1¼-pint jar in hot, soapy water, then rinse well. Place the jar on a baking tray and put it in the oven to dry completely. If using a kilner jar, remove and boil the rubber seal.

2. To make the brine, bring the water and vinegar to the boil in a non-reactive saucepan, then add the salt and stir until dissolved. Remove from the heat, stir in the garlic, coriander seeds and chilli flakes, if using, and leave to cool.

3. Meanwhile, bring a saucepan of salted water to the boil. Add the turnips and simmer for 5 minutes, then drain and leave to cool. Peel them, then cut them into 5-mm/¼-inch slices. Layer the beetroot and turnip slices in the prepared jar.

4. Sieve the cooled brine over the vegetables in the jar, making sure they are submerged – they must not be exposed to air. Tuck in the bay leaf, cover and seal tightly.

5. Set aside in a cool, dark place for 2 days, turning the jar over once each day. Transfer to the refrigerator for 12 days before opening.

Cook's tip: *Pickled green chillies are popular in the Middle East. To make them, follow this recipe, but replace the turnips with 250 g/9 oz green chillies. Halve the amount of the other ingredients.*

Breads &
Savoury
Pastries

Soft pitta bread is made all over the Middle East and eastern Mediterranean. Freshly baked, often several times a day, it is served as an accompaniment to many meals. It is a simple, lightly salted dough and is traditionally baked directly on the bottom of a stone oven.

Pitta Bread

PREP: 30 minutes
RISE: 2 hours 10 minutes
COOK: 10 minutes
MAKES: 6–8

1½ tsp fast-action dried yeast

300 ml/10 fl oz lukewarm water

450 g/1 lb plain flour,
    plus 4 tsp for dusting

1 tbsp vegetable oil,
    plus 1 tsp for oiling

1½ tsp caster sugar

1 tsp sea salt flakes

1. Put the yeast and water in a large bowl and stir until dissolved. Add the flour, oil and sugar, crush in the salt and mix well.

2. Dust a work surface with 1 teaspoon of flour, turn the dough out onto it and knead for 5–10 minutes, or until it is firm. Oil a bowl with ½ teaspoon of oil and put the dough in it. Cover with a damp tea towel and leave to rise in a warm place for 2 hours, or until doubled in size.

3. Preheat the oven to 240°C/475°F/Gas Mark 9. Dust the work surface with 1 teaspoon of flour, turn the dough out onto it and knock it back. Roll it up into a 2-cm/¾-inch thick roll, then cut this into six to eight 1-cm/½-inch wide slices. Roll the slices into balls, cover with a damp tea towel and leave to rise for 10 minutes.

4. Line a baking tray with baking paper, then brush the paper with the remaining oil and dust it with 1 teaspoon of flour. Dust the work surface with the final teaspoon of flour and roll out the balls into 15–20-cm/6–8-inch rounds.

5. Arrange the rounds, spread well apart, on the prepared baking tray. Bake for 10 minutes, or until puffed up. Remove from the oven and cover with a damp tea towel to keep the bread soft.

Cook's tip: To knead dough, fold it in half towards you, press it down using the heel of your hand, lift and rotate a little, then repeat and fold. Try not to add extra flour or oil to stop it sticking to your fingers, as this will affect the texture.

This simple, no-bake, crisp flatbread is a perfect accompaniment for tagines and salads.

Turkish Flatbreads

PREP: 30 minutes
RISE: 1 hour 20 minutes
COOK: 40 minutes
SERVES: 8

750 g/1 lb 10 oz plain flour,
  plus 4 tsp for dusting

1½ tsp fine sea salt

1 tsp ground cumin

½ tsp ground coriander

1 tsp caster sugar

1½ tsp fast-action dried yeast

2 tbsp olive oil, plus 3 tsp

400 ml/14 fl oz lukewarm water

1. Sieve the flour, salt, cumin and coriander together into a large bowl and mix in the sugar and yeast. Make a well in the centre, then stir in the oil and water. Bring everything together into a dough.

2. Dust a work surface with 1 teaspoon of flour, turn the dough out onto it and knead for 5–10 minutes, or until it is smooth and elastic. Oil a bowl with ½ teaspoon of oil and put the dough in it. Cover with a damp tea towel and leave to rise in a warm place for 1 hour, or until smooth and elastic.

3. Dust the work surface with 1 teaspoon of flour, turn the dough out onto it and knock it back. Knead for 1–2 minutes. Line a baking tray with baking paper, then brush the paper with ½ teaspoon of oil and dust it with 1 teaspoon of flour.

4. Divide the dough into eight pieces and roll them into balls. Dust the work surface with the final teaspoon of flour and roll out the balls into 20-cm/8-inch rounds. Cover with a damp tea towel and leave to rise for 20 minutes.

5. Heat a heavy-based frying pan brushed with 1 teaspoon of oil over a medium–high heat. Add a dough round, cover and cook for 2–3 minutes, or until lightly browned on the bottom. Turn over using a fish slice, re-cover the pan and cook for a further 2 minutes, or until lightly browned on the second side. Keep warm while you cook the remaining dough rounds in the same way, adding extra oil when you need it. Serve.

These moreish flatbreads, infused with roast garlic, make a delicious addition to a meze meal. The citrusy sumac combines perfectly with the lemon thyme and salty feta, but you can improvise with your own favourite spice, soft cheese and herb combination if you wish.

Thyme, Feta & Sumac Flatbreads

PREP: 45 minutes
RISE: 1 hour
COOK: 20 minutes
SERVES: 4

6 garlic cloves, unpeeled

5 tbsp olive oil, plus ½ tsp for oiling

1 tsp sea salt flakes

200 ml/7 fl oz lukewarm water

1 tsp runny honey

400 g/14 oz strong white bread flour, plus 3 tsp for dusting

1 tsp fast-action dried yeast

2½ tsp sumac spice

2 tsp fresh lemon thyme leaves, roughly chopped, plus 8 sprigs

75 g/2¾ oz feta cheese, crumbled

2 tbsp extra virgin olive oil

1. Preheat the oven to 180°C/350°F/Gas Mark 4. Coat the garlic with 1 tablespoon of the oil, put it in a small ovenproof dish and roast for 10 minutes. Leave to cool a little, then press the cloves out of their skins into a bowl and mash with the salt. Add the water, honey and 4 tablespoons of oil and mix well. Turn the oven off.

2. Sieve the flour, yeast and 1 teaspoon of sumac into a large bowl and mix in the chopped lemon thyme. Make a well in the centre, then stir in the garlic and water mixture. Bring everything together into a rough dough.

3. Dust a work surface with 1 teaspoon of flour, turn the dough out onto it and knead for 5–10 minutes. Oil a bowl with ½ teaspoon of oil and put the dough in it. Cover with a damp tea towel and leave to rise in a warm place for 45 minutes.

4. Divide the dough into four pieces and roll them into balls. Dust the work surface with 1 teaspoon of flour and roll out each ball into a 10–13-cm/4–5-inch round.

5. Dust a baking tray with the final teaspoon of flour. Arrange the rounds, spread well apart, on the tray. Top each with a quarter of the feta, a sprinkle of sumac and two sprigs of lemon thyme. Leave to rest for 15 minutes. Preheat the oven to 220°C/425°F/Gas Mark 7.

6. Drizzle the breads with the extra virgin olive oil. Bake for 8–10 minutes, or until golden brown and crisp. Serve warm.

Pides

PREP: 25 minutes
RISE: 45 minutes
COOK: 1¼ hours
SERVES: 8

100 g/3½ oz feta cheese, crumbled

Dough

300 g/10½ oz strong white flour,
    plus 2 tsp for dusting

1 tsp fast-action dried yeast

1 tsp caster sugar

200 ml/7 fl oz lukewarm water

2 tbsp extra virgin olive oil, plus
    ½ tsp for oiling

1 tsp fine sea salt, plus a pinch

Roast vegetable filling (optional)

1 red onion, cut into small chunks

1 aubergine, cut into small chunks

2 tbsp olive oil

250 g/9 oz chestnut mushrooms,
    quartered or cut into eighths if large

1 tbsp ras el hanout

2 pinches of sea salt flakes

400 g/14 oz canned chopped tomatoes

4 tbsp roughly chopped fresh coriander

2 tbsp extra virgin olive oil

Spiced sumac meat filling (optional)

1 tbsp olive oil

½ onion, finely chopped

2 garlic cloves, finely chopped

2 tsp sumac spice

1 tsp sea salt flakes

250 g/9 oz fresh beef or lamb mince

400 g/14 oz canned chopped tomatoes

4 tbsp roughly chopped fresh coriander

Pides, or boat-shaped Turkish pizzas, make a versatile and delicious light dinner or lunch. As with Italian pizzas, the choice of topping is only limited by your imagination. You need to prepare just one of these toppings to make eight pides. Alternatively, try roast red peppers and goat's cheese, or wilted spinach, garlic and an egg.

1. For the dough, mix the flour, yeast and sugar together in a large bowl. Make a well in the centre and stir in the water, extra virgin olive oil and 1 teaspoon of salt before bringing everything together into a sticky dough. Dust a work surface with 1 teaspoon of flour, turn the dough out onto it and knead for 5–10 minutes, or until smooth and elastic. Oil a bowl with ½ teaspoon of oil and put the dough in it. Cover with a damp tea towel and leave to rise in a warm place for 45 minutes.

2. If you are making the vegetable filling, preheat your oven to 180°C/350°F/Gas Mark 4. Toss the red onion, aubergine, olive oil, mushrooms, ras el hanout and a pinch of salt together in a roasting tin. Roast for 30 minutes, then tip into a large saucepan. Add the tomatoes, then swirl the tin out with 5 tablespoons of water and pour into the pan. Bring to the boil, then simmer for 30 minutes. Stir in the coriander, extra virgin olive oil and a pinch of salt.

3. If you are making the meat filling, heat the oil in a frying pan over a medium–low heat. Add the onion and garlic and fry for 10 minutes. Reduce the heat to low, then add the sumac and half the salt and fry for 1 minute. Increase the heat to medium, then add the mince and fry for 10 minutes, or until browned, breaking it up using a wooden spoon. Add the tomatoes, then swirl the tin out with 5 tablespoons of water and pour into the pan. Bring to the boil, then simmer for 25 minutes. Stir in the coriander and season with salt.

4. Preheat the oven to its highest setting. Preheat a pizza stone or baking tray on a high shelf. Divide the dough into eight pieces and roll them into balls. Dust the work surface with 1 teaspoon of flour and roll out each ball into a long, flat oblong a few millimetres thick. Place 2 heaped teaspoons of a filling in the centre of each oblong, then pull the long ends up so the filling is encased in a boat shape. Twist each end and sprinkle over the feta. Place the pides directly on the hot pizza stone and bake for 8–10 minutes, or until golden.

Cook's tip: *Put an ovenproof bowl filled with water in the bottom of the oven when baking. This creates steam and gives a good crust.*

These parcels take their inspiration from Turkey, and are best served hot.

Feta & Spinach Filo Parcels

PREP: 25 minutes
COOK: 20 minutes
MAKES: 6

2 tbsp olive oil, plus ½ tsp for oiling

8 spring onions, roughly chopped

500 g/1 lb 2 oz spinach leaves, roughly chopped

1 egg, beaten

125 g/4½ oz feta cheese, crumbled

½ tsp freshly grated nutmeg

pinch of sea salt flakes

pinch of pepper

55 g/2 oz butter

6 sheets of filo pastry, approximately 26 x 29 cm/10½ x 11½ inches

1 tbsp sesame seeds

1. Preheat the oven to 200°C/400°F/Gas Mark 6. Brush a baking tray with the ½ teaspoon of oil.

2. Heat the oil in a wok or large frying pan over a medium heat. Add the spring onions and stir-fry for 1–2 minutes. Add the spinach and stir-fry for 3–4 minutes. Drain off any liquid and leave to cool slightly.

3. Stir the egg, feta, nutmeg, salt and pepper into the spinach mixture. Melt the butter in a small saucepan.

4. Brush three sheets of filo with melted butter. Place another sheet on top of each one and brush with more melted butter. Cut each pair of sheets down the middle to make six long strips in total. Place a tablespoon of the spinach filling on the end of each strip.

5. Lift one corner of filo over the filling to the opposite side, then turn over the opposite way to enclose. Continue to fold over along the length of the strip to make a triangular parcel, finishing with the join underneath.

6. Place the parcels on the prepared baking tray, brush with the remaining melted butter and sprinkle with sesame seeds. Bake for 12–15 minutes, or until golden brown and crisp. Serve hot.

Cook's tip: *When working with filo, keep any unused pastry under a damp, clean tea towel until you are ready to use it, as it dries out very quickly.*

Dates were a staple part of the nomadic Bedouin peoples' diet, even in pre-biblical times. The advanced civilizations that followed replaced the date stone with an expensive whole almond as a culinary joke. These little appetizers go one step further, with the addition of feta and by wrapping the dates in layers of buttered filo pastry.

Date, Almond & Feta Cigars

PREP: 20 minutes
COOK: 20 minutes
SERVES: 8

30 g/1 oz butter

32 whole blanched almonds
  (Marcona, if available)

8 Medjool dates, halved and pitted

150 g/5½ oz feta cheese, crumbled

4 sheets of filo pastry, approximately
  26 x 29 cm/10½ x 11½ inches

1. Preheat the oven to 180°C/350°F/Gas Mark 4. Line a large baking tray with baking paper. Melt the butter in a small saucepan.

2. Push two almonds into the flesh side of each date half. Lay the dates on a work surface, skin side-down. Place a small mound of feta on each, then pat it down; you should have about the same amount of feta as date.

3. Lay a sheet of filo on a work surface and cut it into strips a little wider than the date halves. Place a date half at one end of each strip, then roll the date up in the pastry. Using a pastry brush, brush the end of the filo with melted butter to stick the edge down. Repeat until all the filo and dates have been used up.

4. Place the parcels on the prepared baking tray and brush them well with more melted butter. Bake for 20 minutes, or until crisp and golden. Leave to cool slightly before serving as the date filling gets very hot.

Cook's tip: *Medjool dates are known as the king of dates. They are large and particularly soft, and tend to be grown in the Middle East and North Africa.*

Chicken, Mushroom & Lemon Borekas

PREP: 45 minutes
CHILL: 45 minutes
COOK: 25 minutes
SERVES: 8

Boreka pastry

600 g/1 lb 5 oz plain flour

2 tsp sea salt flakes, crushed

150 ml/5 fl oz olive oil

215 ml/7½ fl oz water

1 egg, lightly beaten, to glaze

Chicken filling

2 tbsp olive oil

300 g/10½ oz chestnut mushrooms,
finely chopped

2 garlic cloves, finely chopped

360 g/12½ oz skinless, boneless
chicken breasts, cut into 1-cm/
½-inch cubes

1 preserved lemon, rinsed and finely
chopped

4 tbsp finely chopped fresh flat-leaf
parsley

juice of 1 lemon

2 tbsp Greek-style natural yogurt

pinch of sea salt flakes

pinch of pepper

Cook's tip: *To freeze, put the filled,
uncooked borekas between sheets of
baking paper, place them in a plastic
box, label and freeze. Defrost them fully
in the refrigerator before baking.*

These Middle Eastern pies combine crisp pastry with a
lemony chicken and mushroom filling. Boreka pastry dough
is tactile and easy to use, and once you've got the hang
of rolling and crimping it, the possibilities for fillings are
endless. These are good as a starter or for a light lunch or
picnic snack.

1. For the pastry, sieve the flour into a large bowl and mix in the
salt. Make a well in the centre and stir in the oil and water using a
fork. Turn the dough out onto a work surface and knead for 20–30
seconds, then bring it together in a flattened disc (it contains a high
proportion of oil so you won't need to flour the surface). Wrap the
dough in clingfilm and chill in the refrigerator for 45 minutes.

2. For the chicken filling, heat the oil in a frying pan over a medium
heat. Add the mushrooms and garlic and fry for 5 minutes, or until
softened. Add the chicken and preserved lemon and fry for 2–3
minutes, stirring. Cover and fry for a further 5 minutes, or until the
chicken is cooked through.

3. Remove the pan from the heat and stir in the parsley and lemon
juice. Leave to cool slightly, then stir in the yogurt, salt and pepper.
Break up any larger chunks of chicken using a wooden spoon, then
leave to cool.

4. Preheat the oven to 200°C/400°F/Gas Mark 6. Line three large
baking trays with baking paper. Divide the boreka dough in half,
then divide these halves in half again, continuing until you have
32 pieces. Roll them into balls and cover them with clingfilm.

5. On a clean, dry work surface, roll one ball into a 7.5-cm/3-inch
diameter circle. Put 2 heaped teaspoons of filling on one side of the
circle, then fold the pastry over into a half-moon shape. Holding
the parcel in one hand, pinch and twist the edges together into an
overlapping 'rope' shape, working clockwise from one side to the
other (alternatively, you can crimp the edges together using a fork).
Transfer to the prepared baking trays. Repeat with the remaining
balls, keeping the unrolled ones covered with clingfilm as you go.

6. Brush the parcels lightly with the beaten egg. Bake for
20–25 minutes, or until golden brown and cooked through. The
borekas are best served hot, but can be served chilled.

Beef Sambousek

PREP: 35 minutes
CHILL: 45 minutes
COOK: 1 hour
SERVES: 8

Boreka pastry

600 g/1 lb 5 oz plain flour

2 tsp sea salt flakes, crushed

150 ml/5 fl oz olive oil

215 ml/7½ fl oz water

1 egg, lightly beaten, to glaze

Beef filling

50 g/1¾ oz pine nuts

2 tbsp olive oil

1 tsp cumin seeds

1 large onion, finely chopped

2 garlic cloves, crushed

1 tsp ground ginger

1 tsp ground cinnamon

1 tsp ground coriander

500 g/1 lb 2 oz fresh beef mince

4 tbsp finely chopped fresh coriander

100 g/3½ oz Greek-style natural yogurt

pinch of sea salt

pinch of pepper

Cook's tip: To freeze, put the filled, uncooked sambousek between sheets of baking paper, place them in a plastic box, label and freeze. Defrost them fully in the refrigerator before baking.

These spiced beef pies, popular in the Lebanon, make excellent snacks or party food. Use finely chopped chestnut mushrooms instead of mince for a vegetarian version. You will need three to four baking sheets.

1. For the pastry, sieve the flour into a large bowl and mix in the salt. Make a well in the centre and stir in the oil and water using a fork. Turn the dough out onto a work surface and knead for 20–30 seconds, then bring it together in a flattened disc (it contains a high proportion of oil so you won't need to flour the surface). Wrap the dough in clingfilm and chill in the refrigerator for 45 minutes.

2. For the beef filling, toast the pine nuts in a frying pan over a medium heat for 2–3 minutes. Tip onto a plate and leave to cool.

3. Heat the oil in the frying pan over a low heat. Add the cumin seeds and fry for 1–2 minutes, or until aromatic. Add the onion, increase the heat to medium, and fry for 10 minutes, or until golden brown, stirring occasionally.

4. Reduce the heat to low, add the garlic, ginger, cinnamon and ground coriander and fry for 2 minutes. Add the mince and fry for 5 minutes, breaking it up well using a wooden spoon. Increase the heat to medium–high and fry for a further 10 minutes, or until well browned, stirring occasionally.

5. Remove the pan from the heat and stir in the toasted pine nuts and fresh coriander. Leave to cool slightly, then stir in the yogurt and salt and pepper to taste.

6. Preheat the oven to 200°C/400°F/Gas Mark 6. Line three large baking trays with baking paper. Divide the boreka dough in half, then divide these halves in half again, continuing until you have 32 pieces. Roll these into balls and cover them with clingfilm.

7. On a clean, dry work surface, roll one ball into a 7.5-cm/3-inch diameter circle (it contains a high proportion of oil so you won't need to flour the surface). Put 2 heaped teaspoons of filling in the centre of the circle, then carefully lift three edges of the pastry up towards the middle and pinch them together to form a three-pointed star. Transfer to the prepared baking trays. Repeat with the remaining dough balls, keeping the unrolled ones covered with clingfilm as you go.

8. Brush the parcels lightly with the beaten egg. Bake for 20–25 minutes, or until golden brown and hot through. These sambousek are best served hot, but can be served chilled.

Chicken Bastilla

PREP: 40 minutes
COOK: 1 hour 10 minutes
SERVES: 4

40 g/1½ oz butter

4 sheets of filo pastry, approximately
    26 x 29 cm/10½ x 11½ inches

2 pinches of sea salt

2 pinches of pepper

60 g/2¼ oz blanched almonds, toasted

1 tbsp icing sugar

½ tsp cinnamon

½ tsp orange flower water

Chicken filling

1 tbsp olive oil

½ onion, finely chopped

pinch of saffron threads

300 ml/10 fl oz boiling water

300 g/10½ oz boneless chicken thighs,
  each cut into eight pieces

juice of ½ lemon

Egg filling

3 eggs, lightly beaten

1 tbsp olive oil

Cook's tip: *If you're serving a crowd, double up the ingredients, using two sheets of filo between each layer. You will need a 23-cm/9-inch dish and you may need to increase the cooking time.*

This traditional Moroccan festival pie combines sweet and savoury ingredients, a classic Middle Eastern technique. The saffron, chicken, eggs and sweet almonds come together in a delicate balance of flavours and textures. Traditionally, fine *warka* pastry is used, but filo works well. It's ideal for a picnic.

1. For the chicken filling, heat the oil in a medium saucepan over a low heat. Add the onion and soften without colouring for 10 minutes.

2. Grind the saffron in a pestle and mortar, then add the boiling water, swirl and tip into a small bowl. Leave to steep. Add the chicken and saffron water to the onion and bring to the boil. Reduce the heat to low and simmer, covered, for 30 minutes, or until the chicken is cooked through.

3. Lift the chicken out of the cooking liquid into a dish using a slotted spoon. Increase the heat to medium–high and boil the liquid until reduced to 4–5 tablespoons of thickened sauce. Stir 2 tablespoons of the sauce into the chicken. Mix in the lemon juice and a pinch of salt and pepper. Cover and leave to cool.

4. For the egg filling, whisk the remaining chicken sauce into the eggs and season with a pinch of salt and pepper. Heat the oil in a saucepan over a low heat. Pour in the eggs and cook, stirring, for 5–6 minutes, or until lightly scrambled. Transfer to a plate and leave to cool.

5. Mix the almonds, icing sugar, cinnamon and orange flower water together in a bowl. Tip into a pestle and mortar and roughly grind.

6. Preheat the oven to 200°C/400°F/Gas Mark 6. To assemble the pie, melt the butter in a small saucepan. Brush a little of the butter around an 18-cm/7-inch round cake tin using a pastry brush. Lay a sheet of pastry over the bottom of the tin, brush with butter, then repeat with two more sheets of pastry in overlapping layers, letting it overhang the sides of the tin.

7. Spread half the egg filling over the filo, top with half the chicken filling, then repeat. Place the remaining filo on top and brush with butter. Spread the almond mixture over this. Fold the edges of the top layer of pastry over the almonds, brush with butter, then fold each original overlapping layer of pastry back over the pie to form a concentric pattern, brushing with butter as you go. Finally, brush the whole pie with butter. Bake for 20 minutes, or until golden brown.

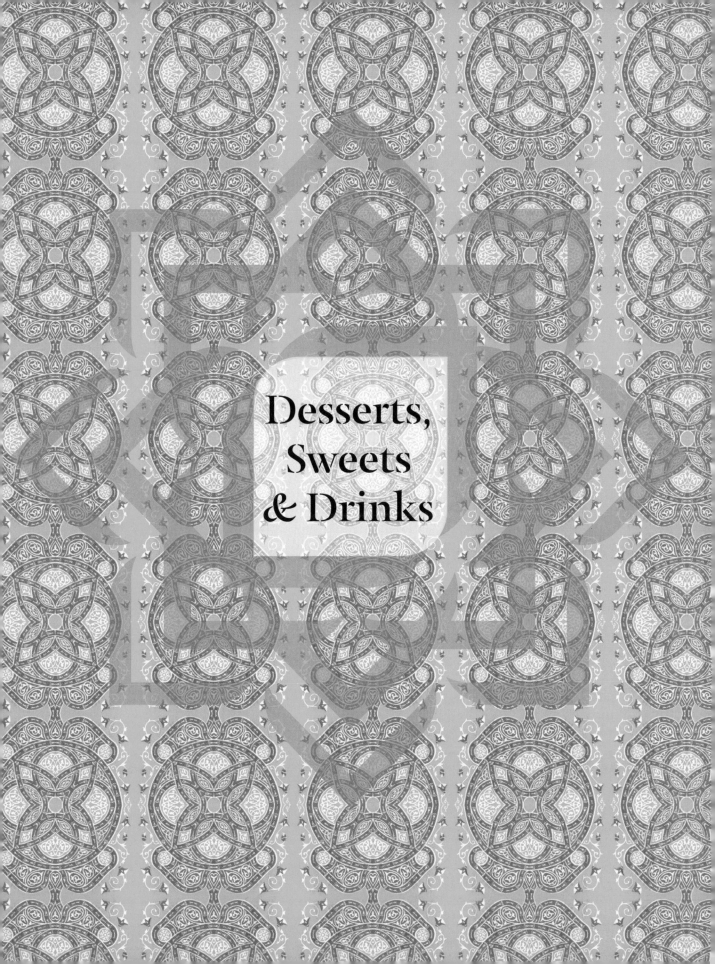

Desserts, Sweets & Drinks

This rich, scented rice pudding is a comforting way to round off a Middle Eastern meal. The syrup adds a hint of sophisticated sweetness that enhances the creaminess of the rice.

Persian Rice Pudding with Rosewater & Cardamom Syrup

PREP: 10 minutes
COOK: 1 hour
SERVES: 4

11 green cardamom pods
100 g/3½ oz basmati rice, rinsed well
750 ml/1¼ pints full-fat milk
¼ tsp rosewater
60 g/2¼ oz golden caster sugar
60 ml/2 fl oz water
1 tsp dried or fresh edible rose petals

1. Split five of the cardamom pods, scrape the seeds into a pestle and mortar and crush them. Tip them into a saucepan.

2. Add the rice, 300 ml/10 fl oz of the milk, the rosewater and 2 teaspoons of the sugar to the pan and stir. Bring to the boil, then reduce the heat to low. Simmer for 1 hour, stirring occasionally and adding an extra ladleful of milk every 10 minutes, or when the rice has absorbed all the milk.

3. When the rice pudding is nearly ready, put the remaining sugar in a separate saucepan with the water, then cook over a medium–low heat until the sugar has dissolved. Add the remaining cardamom pods and the rose petals, then simmer for 2–3 minutes, or until the syrup has thickened.

4. Serve the rice pudding hot, with the syrup drizzled over.

Cook's tip: Cardamom pods come black and green. Black cardamom has a smoky flavour; green has a softer, more balanced flavour.

**Apricots
Poached in
Rosewater &
Cardamom with
Ginger Yogurt**
page 196

This is one of the easiest desserts to make, and the apricots will bring some sunshine to the table. Your guests will be delighted by its exotic fragrance and gently spiced flavour.

Apricots Poached in Rosewater & Cardamom with Ginger Yogurt

PREP: 20 minutes
COOK: 15 minutes
SERVES: 4

150 g/5½ oz caster sugar

6 green cardamom pods, lightly crushed

1 cinnamon stick

¼ tsp rosewater

350 ml/12 fl oz water

4 apricots, halved and stoned

1 tbsp dried edible rose petals, to
   decorate (optional)

Ginger yogurt

100 g/3½ oz Greek-style
   natural yogurt

2.5 cm/1 inch piece of fresh ginger,
   peeled and finely grated

1. Put the sugar, cardamom, cinnamon, rosewater and water in a saucepan, stir and cook over a low heat until the sugar has dissolved.

2. Increase the heat to medium–high, bring to the boil, then lower in the apricots using a slotted spoon. Reduce the heat to low and simmer for 5 minutes. Turn off the heat and leave them in the syrup for 10 minutes.

3. Transfer the apricots to a serving bowl using the slotted spoon. When cool enough to handle, slip off and discard the skins.

4. For the ginger yogurt, put the yogurt in a small serving bowl, stir in the ginger, cover and set aside.

5. Return the syrup to the heat and boil until reduced by half. Pour the syrup over the apricots, then scatter over the dried rose petals, if using. Serve the apricots with the ginger yogurt. If not serving immediately, leave them to cool, then cover and chill in the refrigerator and serve cold.

› **Pictured on previous page**

Cook's tip: Rosewater comes in different strengths, depending on the make. The one used for this recipe was very strong, and the amount gives it a gentle rosiness. Adjust according to your brand and taste.

You don't need to do much with fresh figs, but roasting them brings out their flavour beautifully. This dish is perfect for a smart dinner party dessert, and no one will believe how easy it is to make. Use Greek-style natural yogurt instead of labneh if you are in a hurry.

Roast Figs with Honey & Thyme

PREP: 10 minutes
COOK: 20 minutes
SERVES: 4

8 figs

10 sprigs of fresh thyme, broken into pieces

125 ml/4 fl oz runny honey

100 g/3½ oz labneh, to serve (optional)

1. Preheat the oven to 180°C/350°F/Gas Mark 4. Using a very sharp knife, cut a deep X-shape through each fig, stopping just before the base, and stuff it with two pieces of thyme.

2. Line a small roasting tin with crumpled baking paper, allowing it to come up the sides. Put the figs on the paper, drizzle a tablespoon of honey onto each fig, then scatter over the remaining thyme.

3. Roast the figs for 20 minutes. Serve two figs per person, hot, with the syrup in the baking paper and a generous spoonful of labneh, if using.

› **Pictured overleaf**

Cook's tip: *You can prepare this dessert in advance, then warm it through in the oven at 150°C/300°F/Gas Mark 2 for 10 minutes before serving.*

Roast Figs
with Honey
& Thyme
page 197

People in the Middle East have for centuries packed dates as a provision for travelling through the desert. Here, with pistachio nuts and honey, they are delicious.

Date, Pistachio & Honey Slices

PREP: 30 minutes
COOK: 25 minutes
MAKES: 12

250 g/9 oz dates, stoned and chopped

2 tbsp lemon juice

2 tbsp water

85 g/3 oz pistachio nuts, roughly chopped

2 tbsp runny honey

Pastry

225 g/8 oz plain flour,
   plus 1 tsp for dusting

25 g/1 oz caster sugar

150 g/5 oz cold butter,
   roughly chopped

4–5 tbsp cold water

2 tbsp milk, for glazing

1. Put the dates, lemon juice and water in a saucepan and bring to the boil, stirring. Remove from the heat and stir in the pistachio nuts and 1 tablespoon of the honey. Cover and leave to cool. Preheat the oven to 200°C/400°F/Gas Mark 6.

2. To make the pastry, put the flour, sugar and butter in a food processor and whizz to fine crumbs. Mix in just enough cold water to bind to a soft, not sticky, dough.

3. Lightly dust a work surface with flour. Divide the pastry into two pieces, then roll out each piece to a 30 x 20-cm/12 x 8-inch rectangle. Place a sheet of baking paper on a baking tray and top with a rectangle of pastry. Spread the date mixture to within 1 cm/½ inch of the edge of the pastry, then top with the other rectangle of pastry.

4. Firmly press the edges together, then trim the excess and score the top to mark out 12 slices. Brush with the milk to glaze. Bake for 20–25 minutes, or until golden. Drizzle with the remaining honey and turn out onto a wire rack to cool. Cut into 12 slices and serve.

Cook's tip: *Everything should be cold for pastry making, including your hands and work surface.*

The most evocative of Middle Eastern confectionery, Turkish Delight is headily fragrant, toothachingly sweet and ever-so-slightly addictive.

Easy Turkish Delight

PREP: 20 minutes
COOK: 25 minutes
SET: overnight
SERVES: 6

4 gelatine leaves

200 ml/7 fl oz water

250 g/9 oz granulated sugar

¼ tsp rosewater

a few drops of pink food colouring

1 tbsp cornflour

30 g/1 oz icing sugar

1. Put the gelatine in a shallow bowl, just cover with cold water and leave to soak for 5 minutes.

2. Squeeze the gelatine out well, then put it in a very deep saucepan with the water and place over a low heat until the gelatine has dissolved. Stir in the granulated sugar, rosewater and food colouring, increase the heat to medium–high and bring to the boil. Reduce the heat to low and simmer for 20 minutes without stirring. Boiling sugar is very hot, handle with care and make sure it doesn't bubble over. Add more pink food colouring if you wish.

3. Line a shallow 18-cm/7½-inch square dish or plastic container with heat-safe clingfilm, then pour in the mixture. Leave it to cool to room temperature, then cover with more clingfilm and chill in the refrigerator overnight.

4. The next day, mix the cornflour and icing sugar together on a large, flat plate. Tip the Turkish Delight onto the mixture and carefully peel away the clingfilm. Cut it into squares, coating each one with the icing sugar mixture as you go. Store in a sealed container and eat within a week.

Cook's tip: Traditional Turkish Delight involves stirring the sugar for an hour or more, so this cheat's method is a real time saver.

Wonderfully easy to make, these little clouds of lightly whipped cream look beautiful piled into your prettiest glasses. Your guests will love their Middle Eastern scent of cinnamon and orange flower water.

Cinnamon-spiced Syllabub

PREP: 10 minutes
CHILL: 1 hour
SERVES: 8

juice of 2 lemons

½ tsp ground cinnamon, plus a
    pinch to decorate

1 tsp orange flower water

100 g/3½ oz caster sugar

600 ml/1 pint double cream

1 tbsp chopped pistachios,
    to decorate

2 tbsp pomegranate seeds, to decorate

1. Put the lemon juice, cinnamon, orange flower water and sugar in a large bowl and whisk briefly to dissolve the sugar. Add the cream and lightly whisk until it just comes together as barely solid – this should take no more than 1 minute.

2. Spoon the syllabub into eight small 100 ml/3½ fl oz glasses. Sprinkle with the remaining cinnamon, the pistachios and pomegranate seeds. Cover and chill in the refrigerator for at least 1 hour, or up to a day. Serve cold.

Cook's tip: *Syllabub should not be the texture of trifle topping, so be careful not to overwhisk it after adding the cream.*

Sometimes the simplest things are the best.
The sticky tahini and date syrup perfectly complements the firm bananas.

Banana Flatbreads with Tahini & Date Syrup

PREP: 10 minutes
COOK: 5 minutes
SERVES: 4

4 x 20-cm/8-inch wholemeal tortillas

4 tbsp tahini

3 tbsp date syrup

4 bananas, peeled

1. Preheat a frying pan over a medium–high heat. Add a tortilla and warm for 1 minute, turning halfway.

2. Arrange the tortilla on a chopping board, thinly spread it with a quarter of the tahini, then drizzle with a quarter of the date syrup. Add a banana, just a little off-centre, then roll up tightly. Repeat with the remaining tortillas.

3. Cut each tortilla into thick slices, secure each slice with a cocktail stick and arrange on a plate. Serve warm.

Cook's tip: *Store your tahini upside down when you first buy it – it makes stirring it much easier.*

These chunky, nutty bars use traditional Middle Eastern ingredients in a modern way to create a delicious raw snack.

Date & Coconut Bars

PREP: 30 minutes
CHILL: 3 hours
MAKES: 12

400 g/14 oz Medjool dates, halved and stoned

60 g/2¼ oz unblanched almonds

60 g/2¼ oz cashew nut pieces

35 g/1¼ oz chia seeds

2 tsp vanilla extract

2 tbsp maca (optional)

20 g/¾ oz desiccated coconut

55 g/2 oz unblanched hazelnuts, roughly chopped

25 g/1 oz pecan nuts, broken in half

1. Put the dates, almonds and cashew pieces in a food processor and whizz until finely chopped.

2. Add the chia seeds, vanilla extract and maca, if using, and whizz until the mixture binds together into a rough ball.

3. Put a sheet of baking paper on a work surface and sprinkle with half the coconut. Put the date ball on top, then press it into a roughly shaped rectangle. Cover with a second sheet of baking paper and roll out to a 30 x 20-cm/12 x 8-inch rectangle. Lift off the top piece of paper, sprinkle with the remaining coconut, the hazelnuts and pecan nuts, then re-cover with the paper and briefly roll out to press the nuts into the date mixture.

4. Loosen the top paper and transfer the date mixture, still on the base paper, to a tray. Chill for 3 hours, or overnight, until firm.

5. Remove the top paper, cut the date mixture into 12 pieces and peel off the base paper. Pack the date bars into a plastic container, layering with pieces of baking paper to keep them separate. Store in the refrigerator for up to 3 days.

Cook's tip: *Maca is a root belonging to the radish family. It's not traditionally Middle Eastern and isn't essential to these bars, but it is considered to be a superfood and makes a healthy addition to this snack.*

Persian Love Cake

PREP: 45 minutes
COOK: 20 minutes
COOL: 1 hour
SERVES: 10

225 g/8 oz soft light brown sugar

225 g/8 oz unsalted butter, softened, plus ½ tsp for greasing

4 eggs

165 g/5¾ oz self-raising flour

65 g/2¼ oz ground almonds

½ tsp ground cinnamon

6 green cardamom pods, seeds only

Rose mascarpone frosting

750 g/1 lb 10 oz mascarpone

150 g/5½ oz icing sugar

¼ tsp rosewater

a few drops of pink food colouring (optional)

40 g/1½ oz pistachio nuts, roughly chopped

1 tbsp dried or fresh edible rose petals, to decorate (optional)

Love cake, according to legend, was made by a love-struck woman for a Persian prince, who promptly (and sensibly) fell in love with her upon eating it. There are numerous variations on Persian love cake, from dense, heavily spiced almond cakes, to fluffy angel food-style chiffon cakes, to rubbly nut-based yogurt cheesecakes. This delicate, carefully spiced layer cake, with a rose-scented mascarpone frosting, incorporates elements from all of these.

1. Preheat the oven to 180°C/350°F/Gas Mark 4. Grease three 20-cm/8-inch round springform cake tins with butter and line them with baking paper.

2. Using an electric hand whisk or wooden spoon, beat the soft light brown sugar and butter together in a large bowl until well mixed. Beat in the eggs, one at a time, whisking well after each addition. If the mixture looks like it will split, sprinkle a little of the flour in with each egg.

3. In a separate bowl, mix the flour, almonds and cinnamon together. Crush the cardamom seeds in a pestle and mortar, then stir them into the flour mixture.

4. Fold the flour mixture into the whisked eggs and sugar until incorporated. Divide the mixture equally between the three tins, level out the tops and bake for 20 minutes. To check the cakes are cooked, insert a skewer into each one – it should come out clean. Leave the cakes to cool in their tins for 10 minutes, then transfer them to a wire rack and leave to cool completely.

5. Once the cakes have cooled, make the frosting. Using an electric hand whisk or wooden spoon, beat the mascarpone in a large bowl briefly until smooth. Whisk in the icing sugar, rosewater and enough food colouring, if using, to give a very pale pink colour. Spoon the icing into a piping bag fitted with a plain nozzle.

6. Pipe one-third of the icing over one of the cakes in small minaret-shaped rounds, then sprinkle with pistachios. Add another cake and pipe over half the remaining icing in rounds, followed by more pistachios. Add the final cake, then pipe rounds over it in a design of your choice, before sprinkling with the remaining pistachios and the rose petals, if using.

Cook's tip: *The cake will keep for several hours at room temperature, but any leftovers should be refrigerated.*

Warm Walnut & Orange Cake

PREP: 45 minutes
COOK: 2¼ hours
SERVES: 10

3 large whole oranges
(about 250 g/9 oz each)

125 g/4½ oz dried apricots

70 g/2½ oz walnuts, roughly chopped,
plus 12 halves to decorate

70 g/2½ oz unblanched almonds,
roughly chopped, plus 6 whole
to decorate

70 g/2½ oz Brazil nuts, roughly chopped,
plus 12 whole to decorate

4 eggs

200 g/7 oz caster sugar

125 ml/4 fl oz light olive oil,
plus ½ tsp for greasing

85 g/3 oz brown rice flour

2 tsp gluten-free baking powder

250 g/9 oz low-fat Greek-style natural
yogurt, to serve

The classic orange cake is one of the most popular Middle Eastern treats. The whole cooked orange gives this one a tangy citrus hit – and it's gluten-free, too.

1. Put one orange in a small saucepan, just cover with water, then bring to the boil, cover and simmer for 45 minutes. Add the dried apricots, re-cover and cook for 15 minutes, or until the orange is very tender when pierced with a knife. Drain the fruits, reserving the cooking water, and leave to cool.

2. Preheat the oven to 160°C/325°F/Gas Mark 3. Lightly brush a 24-cm/9½-inch round springform cake tin with oil. Put the 70 g/2½ oz each of walnuts, almonds and Brazil nuts in a food processor, then whizz until finely ground. Transfer to a large mixing bowl.

3. Roughly chop the cooked orange, discard any pips, then put it and the apricots in the food processor and whizz into a coarse purée. Add the eggs, 150 g/5½ oz sugar and the oil, and whizz until smooth.

4. Spoon the brown rice flour and baking powder into the ground nuts and mix well. Tip into the food processor with the purée and whizz briefly, until smooth. Pour the cake mixture into the prepared tin, spread it level using a spatula, and decorate with the walnut halves, whole almonds and whole Brazil nuts.

5. Bake for 1–1¼ hours, or until browned, slightly cracked on top, and a skewer inserted into the centre comes out clean. Check after 40 minutes and loosely cover the top with foil if the nut decoration is browning too quickly.

6. Meanwhile, cut the peel and pith away from the remaining two oranges using a small serrated knife. Cut between the membranes to release the segments. Measure 125 ml/4 fl oz of the reserved orange cooking water, making it up with extra water if necessary, and pour it into a small saucepan. Add the remaining sugar and cook over a low heat until the sugar has dissolved. Increase the heat to high and boil for 3 minutes, or until you have a syrup. Add the orange segments and leave to cool.

7. Loosen the edge of the cake with a round-bladed knife and turn it out onto a wire rack. Leave to cool slightly, then cut into wedges and serve warm, with the oranges in syrup and Greek yogurt.

Baklava, a rich, sweet pastry made with filo, filled with nuts and sweetened with either syrup or honey, is popular in Middle Eastern cuisine. This recipe is for the Turkish version, and is made with honey and walnuts. It is popular on feast days.

Baklava

PREP: 45 minutes
COOK: 40 minutes
MAKES: 30

400 g/14 oz finely chopped mixed
    nuts, such as walnuts, almonds,
    pistachio nuts
175 g/6 oz butter, plus ½ tsp for greasing
14 sheets filo pastry, approximately
    26 x 29 cm/10½ x 11½ inches
2 tbsp caster sugar
1 tsp ground cinnamon

Syrup
325 g/11½ oz caster sugar
300 ml/10 fl oz water
1 tbsp lemon juice
3 tbsp runny honey
2 small cinnamon sticks

1. Preheat the oven to 180°C/350°F/Gas Mark 4. Line a baking tray with baking paper. Spread the nuts on the prepared tray and bake for 5–10 minutes. Do not turn off the oven.

2. Meanwhile, melt the butter in a small saucepan. Grease a 25 x 35-cm/10 x 14-inch baking tin with melted butter and place one sheet of filo on top. (Cover the unused sheets with a damp tea towel to prevent them drying out.) Brush the filo with melted butter. Continue layering the filo and brushing with melted butter until there are five layers of filo in the tin.

3. Mix the nuts with the sugar and ground cinnamon. Sprinkle one third of the mixture over the filo, then cover with two more buttered layers of filo. Sprinkle half the remaining nut mixture over the filo and cover with two more layers of buttered filo. Sprinkle the remaining nut mixture over the pastry, cover with five layers of buttered filo and fold in all the overhanging edges. Using a sharp knife, cut the baklava into diamond shapes, slicing through all the layers, then bake for 25–30 minutes, or until golden brown.

4. Meanwhile, make the syrup. Put the sugar and water in a saucepan, stir and place over a low heat until the sugar has dissolved. Increase the heat to medium, bring to the boil, then add the lemon juice, honey and cinnamon sticks. Reduce the heat to low and simmer for 10 minutes. Remove from the heat and leave to cool.

5. Pour the syrup over the baklava and leave to stand until the filo has absorbed all the syrup. The flavour of the baklava will mature for 1–2 days.

Sherbet, or *sharbat*, is a popular soft drink in the Middle East. It is a sweet cordial made from fresh flower petals or fruit, and here it is served as a long drink, diluted to taste with still or sparkling water. It can also be served over crushed ice and eaten with a spoon. This pomegranate and rosewater version is good with gin.

Pomegranate & Rose Sherbet Drink

PREP: 10 minutes
COOK: 6 minutes
SERVES: 8–10

juice of 2 lemons

¼ tsp rosewater

200 ml/7 fl oz fresh pomegranate juice (juice of about 2 pomegranates)

200 g/7 oz caster sugar

crushed ice, to serve

8 fresh mint sprigs, to serve (optional)

sparkling or still water, to serve

1. Put the lemon juice, rosewater, pomegranate juice and sugar in a saucepan, stir and cook over a low heat until the sugar has dissolved.

2. Increase the heat to medium–high, bring to the boil, then reduce the heat to low and simmer for 3–4 minutes. Boiling sugar is very hot, handle with care and make sure it doesn't bubble over. Leave to cool completely.

3. Put some crushed ice in a tall glass. Pour a dash of the cordial over the ice and add a sprig of mint, if using. Pour in still or sparkling water to taste, mix well and serve.

4. The syrup will keep in the refrigerator in a sealed container for 3–4 days.

Cook's tip: To extract the juice from a pomegranate, cut it into eight segments, then squeeze each segment into a sieve set over a bowl. Use the back of a spoon to extract the juice from any whole seeds that fall into the sieve. For a more floral sherbet, increase the amount of rosewater drop by drop, tasting all the time; it can be overpowering if used too liberally.

Mint Tea

PREP: 10 minutes
SERVES: 4

2 tsp Chinese gunpowder green tea
1 small bunch of fresh mint leaves
4 tsp caster sugar

This refreshing tea is Morocco's national drink, offered just about everywhere you go. It is also served at the end of a meal. It is prepared by brewing Chinese gunpowder green tea with fresh mint sprigs.

1. Warm a teapot by adding a little hot water, swirling it around and then discarding the water. Put the tea in the pot, then add the mint, reserving four sprigs, and sugar.

2. Pour in enough boiling water to make four cups of tea and stir once, then leave to infuse for 5 minutes. Pour into four tea glasses or cups and serve decorated with the reserved mint sprigs.

Apple & Tahini Juice

PREP: 10 minutes
SERVES: 1

2 apples, halved

1 small banana, peeled and
  roughly chopped

2 tbsp natural yogurt

1 tbsp light tahini

½ tsp sesame seeds,
  to decorate

The banana and tahini gives this drink a distinctive Middle Eastern flavour. It's ideal for a mid-morning pick-me-up or as a liquid breakfast.

1. Feed the apples through a juicer. Pour the juice into a blender, add the banana, yogurt and tahini and whizz until smooth. Pour into a glass, sprinkle with sesame seeds and serve.

Cook's tip: *If you don't have a juicer, you will need 125 ml/4 fl oz fresh apple juice.*

For a sharp, refreshing drink on a hot summer's day, you can't do much better than a jug of fresh home-made lemonade. In this recipe the rosewater adds a lovely floral twist.

Rose Lemonade

PREP: 15 minutes
COOK: 15 minutes
CHILL: 1 hour
SERVES: 4

finely grated zest of 2 unwaxed lemons

½ tsp rosewater

250 g/9 oz caster sugar

250 ml/9 fl oz water

350 ml/12 fl oz lemon juice (juice of about 10 lemons)

600 ml/1 pint iced water

small pinch of sea salt

4 tbsp fresh pomegranate juice

crushed ice, to taste

4 lemon slices, to serve

1. Put the lemon zest, rosewater, sugar and water in a saucepan. Cook over a medium–low heat, stirring continuously, until the sugar has dissolved. Leave to cool.

2. To make up the lemonade, pour 300 ml/10 fl oz of the lemon juice into a jug, add three-quarters of the sugar syrup, 400 ml/14 fl oz of the iced water and the salt and stir well. Taste, then add more iced water to dilute, more sugar syrup for sweetness or more lemon juice for sharpness, according to taste.

3. To colour the lemonade pink, stir in the pomegranate juice. Cover and chill in the refrigerator for at least 1 hour.

4. To serve the lemonade, divide the crushed ice between four glasses, then pour over the lemonade and add a slice of lemon.

Cook's tip: *The lemonade will intensify in flavour as it chills, so you may wish to dilute it a little further with iced water before serving from the fridge. If you accidentally over-dilute it when making up the lemonade, and you can wait a few hours before serving it, just pop it in the fridge until it has the right flavour balance.*

Index